SCAFFOLDING LANGUAGE, SCAFFOLDING LEARNING

Teaching Second Language Learners in the Mainstream Classroom

PAULINE GIBBONS

Foreword by Jim Cummins

HEINEMANN
Portsmouth, NH

Heinemann

361 Hanover Street
Portsmouth, NH 03801–3912
www.heinemann.com

Offices and agents throughout the world

Library of Congress Cataloging-in-Publication Data
Gibbons, Pauline, 1946–
 Scaffolding language, scaffolding learning : teaching second language learners in the mainstream classroom / Pauline Gibbons ; foreword by Jim Cummins.
  p. cm.
 Includes bibliographical references and index.
 ISBN 0-325-00366-1 (pbk. : acid-free paper)
 1. English language—Study and teaching—Foreign speakers. 2. Interdisciplinary approach in education. 3. Second language acquisition. 4. Language and education. I. Title.

 PE1128.A2 G48 2002
 428'.0071—dc21   2001007440

Editor: Danny Miller
Production: Vicki Kasabian
Cover design: Jenny Jensen Greenleaf
Typesetter: Argosy
Manufacturing: Steve Bernier/Jamie Carter

Printed in the United States of America on acid-free paper
10 09 08   VP   14 15 16

Contents

Foreword

Rarely has education been so high on the agenda of policy makers and politicians around the world as during the past fifteen years. Many countries that formerly operated a relatively decentralized school system with considerable local autonomy to achieve curriculum goals have now "tightened up" and imposed, as a condition of funding, standards that must be achieved and instructional methods that must be followed. Attainment of these standards is increasingly monitored by means of high-stakes standardized tests, with rewards and punishments meted out to schools and educators on the basis of students' performance. Predictably the jargon has proliferated: in addition to *standards*, we have *performance indicators, benchmarks, outcomes-based education, quality assurance, attainment targets, minimal competency testing, accountability*, and so forth. Intense debate has occurred not only about the consequences of high-stakes testing (e.g., the dangers of teaching to the test) but also about topics such as appropriate methods for teaching reading and the efficacy or otherwise of bilingual education as a means of promoting achievement among English language learners (ELL).

The standards-based reform movement has been fueled by parallel developments in many countries. The common context is one where educational systems are attempting to redefine themselves in light of rapidly changing economic, technological, and social conditions that are affecting countries around the world. The shift from an industrialized to a knowledge-based economy has highlighted the need for workers with higher levels of literacy and numeracy than was previously the case.

Complicating the process of top-down reform has been the rapid escalation of linguistic and cultural diversity in many countries. Imposition of a one-size-fits-all standard in curriculum content areas becomes highly problematic in a context where a significant number of students (e.g., at least 25 percent in states such as California) are in the process of acquiring basic knowledge of the language of instruction. As Pauline Gibbons notes, the research is very clear that ELL students require considerably more time to catch up to grade expectations in the academic registers of English as compared to the conversational registers (typically at least five years as compared to less than two years). Too often students are left to fend for themselves after they have attained basic conversational fluency, and many continue to experience academic difficulty.

Fortunately, in this book Pauline Gibbons has given us clear directions and classroom-tested strategies for supporting students' academic progress beyond the initial stages of acquiring English. We see how the teaching of language can be integrated seamlessly with the teaching of content and how academic achievement can be boosted without sacrificing our own vision of education to the dictates of knee-jerk accountability.

A standardized test may provide some perspective on the present level of academic functioning of a particular student or school (even this is hotly debated). However, it is clearly illegitimate logically and meaningless from a policy perspective to make inferences regarding student progress or quality of instruction on the basis of comparisons between schools whose student composition varies enormously—for example, suburban schools whose students are predominantly native English-speakers and inner-city schools whose students are predominantly learners of English. A typical student who has been learning English for only one or two years will inevitably perform more poorly on standardized tests than one whose native language is English. This pattern of test performance says nothing about the quality of instruction that each student has received. However, the awkward presence of ELL students has not been permitted to slow down the accountability juggernaut in North America or elsewhere.

In contrast to many of the politicians, teachers of ELL students see very clearly that high-stakes testing can give a highly misleading picture of both student progress and the quality of instruction in schools that have significant numbers of ELL students. Yet teachers frequently have to function in contexts where their voices regarding the needs of their students are ignored. In some school districts, the educational response to linguistic diversity has been to insist on teaching even more intensively to the test. Skills-oriented transmission approaches to instruction have submerged the fragile rhetoric of the need for higher-order thinking and critical literacy. In some inner-city districts, "teacher-proof" scripted phonics programs that reduce teachers' instructional role simply to parroting the one-size-fits-all script have been presented as a quick fix to boosting students' reading and overall academic progress.

What are the consequences for students and teachers of the regime of top-down standards and high-stakes standardized testing? What is left out of students' educational experience that as a society we might consider valuable? What types of classroom interactions that we previously considered central to developing ELL students' academic language will now be dumped in the "off-task" trash bin? What is the image of the teacher as educator, and student as learner, implied by this approach?

Clearly, these new realities reflect a profound distrust of teachers and an extremely narrow interpretation of the teaching-learning process. Nowhere in this anemic instructional vision is there room for really connecting at a human level with culturally diverse students; consigned to irrelevance also is any notion of affirming students' identities by activating what they already know about the world and mobilizing the intellectual and linguistic tools they use to make sense of their worlds. Test-driven curricula reduce instruction to a technical exercise. No role is envisaged for teachers or students to invest their identities (affect, intellect, and imagination) collaboratively in the teaching-learning process.

Within this context of simplistic technocratic attempts to solve educational problems, Pauline Gibbons' book emerges as an eloquent reaffirmation of the central role that teachers play in creating classroom contexts that foster their students' academic, linguistic, and personal growth. In lucid prose, she demystifies what is involved in promoting conversational and academic language proficiency among ELL students and gives us a sense of how exciting and personally rewarding this challenge can be for both teachers and students. In contrast to prescriptions to teach skills and content as part of a one-way transmission process, teaching and learning are conceived as an integrated *social* process. Teachers and students are active participants in this process, and learning is seen as a collaborative endeavor. Skills, content knowledge, and student identities emerge and become shaped in the flow of teacher-student interaction.

As the title of the book indicates, *scaffolding* is a central notion in the teaching-learning framework that Pauline Gibbons articulates. Drawing on theoretical constructs advanced by Lev Vygotsky in relation to the nature of learning and by Michael Halliday regarding registers of language, she highlights how teachers and students work together, through their classroom interaction, to develop new skills, concepts, and levels of understanding. This support, or scaffolding, enables children to perform tasks independently that previously they could perform only with the assistance or guidance of the teacher. Rich examples of classroom discourse throughout the book illustrate exactly how this scaffolding process works and how much it draws on teachers' intuition, sensitivity, and feeling for language. Formulaic it is not, unlike the "teacher-proof" scripts that are increasingly being foisted on teachers and students in inner-city schools.

Throughout the book there is an emphasis on providing explicit information to students about the nature of particular linguistic genres and the "rules of the game" that operate with different text types. It is equally important to demystify in an explicit way concepts and semantic relationships that operate in particular content areas. However, this explicitness is part of a process whereby knowledge is co-constructed between teachers and students. Task-focused student talk and writing—collaborative use of language—is the medium through which students' knowledge of the world and knowledge about language emerges.

Within the pedagogy articulated in this volume, ELL students are constructed as active seekers after meaning who are capable of motivated inquiry, insight, and intelligence. Teachers are similarly constructed as professionals capable of making creative links between theory and practice and between practice and theory. The respect for teachers and students that is communicated on every page of this book is a far cry from current trends that conceive of education as a form of "service delivery" to be evaluated by standardized tests on the basis of its "productivity."

I hope that this book is read widely by "mainstream" classroom teachers as well as by those directly involved in English language teaching to ELL students. Increasingly, this mainstream classroom is populated by students from around the globe who bring to the classroom diverse and rich experiences together with specific learning needs. It is no longer enough to see ourselves as competent and committed teachers in a generic sense. The "generic" student is no longer white, middle-class, monolingual, and monocultural. Instead, students in our classrooms come from many different national and cultural backgrounds, speak and understand a good sample of the languages of the world, and require specific kinds of instruction to enable them to reach their full potential as human beings.

This book is a great place to start in exploring the kinds of instruction that will fully promote ELL students' linguistic and academic potential. Not only is it concise, accessible, and eminently practical, but more fundamentally, it communicates an exuberance about education while reaffirming teachers' commitment to nurture the intellectual and linguistic resources that students bring to the classroom, and from there to our societies. It articulates a clear and unpretentious sense of what education is all about, one that is focused on harnessing children's power to use language as the primary tool for intellectual and academic development. The interpersonal and collaborative spaces created in the classroom between teachers and students by these powerful uses of language are much closer to our intuitive sense of what education ought to be than the constricted focus that dominates so many current policy discussions.

The difficult times in which we live demand that our classrooms nurture thinking and creative problem-solving abilities as well as sensitivity to the perspectives of those from diverse cultural and linguistic backgrounds. Only in these kinds of instructional spaces will language, learning, and academic abilities truly develop. Only in classroom contexts where ELL students' brainpower is fully acknowledged and activated will they catch up rapidly to their peers in academic performance. The theory and practice described so clearly by Pauline Gibbons in this volume highlight how to create these spaces in our own classrooms for all of our students.

Jim Cummins
The University of Toronto

Acknowledgments

The ideas presented in this book have evolved over many years. I owe a significant debt to the hundreds of teachers with whom I have worked during that time; I have learned much from their practices and been challenged by their questions.

Thanks are also due to my wonderful colleagues at the University of Technology, Sydney, for their feedback, encouragement, and friendship.

I would also like to thank my son Mark. I appreciate his special brand of humor and his cartoons have enlivened the pages of this book.

I would like especially to express my appreciation and thanks to Danny Miller, whose editorial guidance, encouraging comments, and enthusiasm for the book have made the writing of it a pleasure.

Finally, my thanks to Jim Cummins, whose work with minority children has been an inspiration and has long influenced my own work, for writing the foreword, and for the initial suggestion that I write this book.

1

Scaffolding Language and Learning

"I can say what I want, but not for school work and strangers." English language learner quoted in McKay, Davies, Devlin, Clayton, Oliver, and Zammit, *The Bilingual Interface Project Report*

ESL Students in the Mainstream Classroom

The comment in the epigraph was made by an eleven-year-old girl for whom English was a second language. She had been asked, "How good do you think your English is?" Her response suggests that while she feels able to communicate in general terms, she is less confident when it comes to using English at school, or with people with whom she is not on familiar terms. This may not seem surprising—it requires more linguistic skills to use language for academic purposes than it does to use it in everyday conversation. Similarly, if we are using a second language, it is often easier to talk to people we know well and with whom we are at ease than to converse more formally with a stranger. What is more surprising about this comment is that this student—let's call her Julianna—was born in Australia and has been exposed to English throughout her primary education. She began school at age five, as fluent as any other five-year-old in her mother tongue but speaking little English. Now, six years later, she feels that her English is still inadequate for certain purposes.

Why should this be? Surely, it could be argued, six years is sufficient time to learn a new language, given the fact that Julianna has been living in an English-speaking country and attending an English-medium school. Like many second language learners, she also appears to her teachers to speak English as fluently as her English-speaking peers. But Julianna is not unusual: many second language learners seem able to cope with English at school, yet have academic or literacy-related difficulties in class. To understand why this might be, we need to think about the nature of language, and in particular how it varies according to the context in which it is used.

Language and Context

The theory of language on which this book draws is based on the work of Michael Halliday and other linguists working within systemic functional linguistics. These linguists argue that language is involved in almost everything we do, and whenever we use language there is a context, or to be more precise, two kinds of context. There is, first, a *context of culture*: speakers within a culture share particular assumptions and expectations, so that they are able to take for granted the ways in which things are done. Knowing how to greet someone, how to order a meal in a restaurant, how to participate in a class, or how to write a business letter are examples of this kind of cultural knowledge. While cultures may share many common purposes for using language, how these things actually get done varies from culture to culture.

A second kind of context is the *context of situation*, the particular occasion on which the language is being used. One of the most fundamental features of language is that *it varies according to the context of situation*. This context is characterized by three features: (1) what is being talked (or written) about; (2) the relationship between the speakers (or writer and reader); and (3) whether the language is spoken or written. How we use language is determined largely by these contextual features. Think, for example, of the differences between a conversation about teaching and one about cooking, or between a social studies text and a biology text. Imagine yourself chatting to a friend at a party and compare that with how you might respond to questions at a job interview. Or think about how differently language might be used during a computer demonstration compared to the way the same information might be written in a computer manual.

Halliday and Hasan (1985) refer to these contextual factors as *field, tenor,* and *mode*. Thus:

- *Field* refers to the topic of the text.
- *Tenor* refers to the relationship between speaker and listener (or writer and reader).
- *Mode* refers to the channel of communication.

Together these three variables constitute what is referred to as the *register* of a text. As children learn their first language, they gradually learn to vary the language they use according to the context they are in. In other words, they learn to vary the *register* of the language so that it is appropriate for the context.

The ability to handle register is a developmental process for children learning their first language. One of the first things a young child learns to do is to talk about the "here and now"—to refer to the objects and goings-on in their immediate environment. Here-and-now language occurs in contexts where both speakers can see each other, and where there are visual clues, gestures, and facial expressions to help communication. Often what is being talked about is embedded in the visual context, such as "Put it there." If we are not present we don't know what *it* and *there* refer to. Similarly, if we are speaking on the phone, we have to express this differently, with more details: "Put the television in the corner." But the words *it* and *there* would be perfectly understandable to speakers who could see what was being referred to.

As children get older, they gradually become able to use language in a more explicit or abstract way to refer to things that aren't in their immediate surroundings, such as to tell someone about what happened at kindergarten that day. They may not always be successful at first. If you talk with very young children, you'll notice that they do not always provide enough information for you to understand them if you did not share the experience they are referring to, and you are left wondering what exactly they are trying to tell you. Halliday (1993) refers to this as the ability to "impart meanings which are not already known" (102). He writes:

> When children are first using language to annotate and classify experience, the particular experience that is being construed in any utterance is one that the addressee is known to have shared. When the child says *green bus*, the context is "that's a green bus; you saw it too." . . . What the child cannot do at this stage is to impart the experience to someone who has not shared it. [At a later stage] children learn to tell people things they do not already know. (102)

Making Meaning Explicit

Martin (1984) suggests that "the more speakers are doing things together and engaging in dialogue, the more they can take for granted. As language moves away from the events it describes, and the possibility of feedback is removed, more and more of the meanings must be made explicit in the text" (27). Here, the term *text* refers to a piece of complete meaningful language, both spoken and written. In other words, the language itself must contain more information because it cannot depend on the addressee knowing exactly what occurred. Consider the differences between these four texts:

- Look, it's making them move. Those didn't stick.
- We found out the pins stuck on the magnet.
- Our experiment showed that magnets attract some metals.
- Magnetic attraction occurs only between ferrous metals.

Here we can see how the register of each text changes because the context in which it was produced is different: each text is more explicit than the one that precedes it. Text 1 was spoken by a child talking in a small group as they were experimenting with a magnet to find out which objects it attracted. Without knowing this, it's hard to work out what's being talked about—we don't know what *them* and *those* are referring to, and the words *move* and *stick* could occur in a number of different contexts. Text 1 demonstrates how dependent "here-and-now" language is on the immediate situational context. Text

2 is the same child telling the teacher what she had learned, and is in the form of a recount in which *the pins* and *the magnet* refer to specific objects. These words make the text more explicit and therefore easier to understand. Text 3 is from her written report and contains a generalization: *magnets attract some metals*. The text is starting to sound more scientific. For example, *stick* is replaced by *attract*. Text 4, by way of comparison, is from a child's encyclopedia. The language is much denser, and the process to which the child was referring in Texts 1, 2, and 3 is now summarized in the notion of *magnetic attraction*.

While the *field* of all four texts is the same (i.e., they are on the same topic), there are considerable differences in the way in which the language is used. As they begin to refer to events not shared by listeners or readers, the vocabulary becomes more technical and subject or *field* specific; the *tenor* of the texts becomes more impersonal (notice how the personal reference to *we* and *our* disappear), and the *mode* varies (they become increasingly more explicit and more like written language). Of course, we could continue this continuum; imagine, for example, how magnetism might be written about in a university book on physics. In many ways, this set of texts reflects the process of formal education: as children move through school, they are expected to progress from talking only about their here-and-now personal experiences toward using the particular registers of different curriculum areas, and expressing increasingly more abstract ideas.

The four texts demonstrate how it is problematic to talk about overall "proficiency" in a language without taking into account the context in which the language will be used. As Baynham (1993) suggests, language learning is not a simple linear process but a "functional diversification, an extension of a learner's communicative range" (5). Even a fluent mother-tongue speaker of English will not be proficient in every possible context: for example, there will always be some subjects that they know very little about and so can't talk about. Or perhaps there is a particular form of writing, such as a Ph.D. proposal, that even highly educated people might not be familiar with and would need guidance in producing. So it is not simply a matter of getting the basic "grammar" correct, but of knowing the most *appropriate* language to use in the context.

Learning New Registers

So what has all this to do with Julianna, the student quoted at the beginning of the chapter? It is obvious that a second language learner is likely to have far fewer difficulties in producing something like Text 1, where the visual context provides a support for meaning making, and where fewer linguistic resources are required, than with subsequent texts that require increasingly more control over grammar and vocabulary. Cummins (1996, 2000) uses the terms *context-embedded* and *context-reduced* to refer to the distinction between the registers of everyday language and the more academic registers of school, and has suggested that whereas a second language learner is likely to develop conversational language quite rapidly—usually taking between one and two years—the registers associated with academic learning take between five and seven years for the learner to develop at a level equivalent to a competent native speaker of the same age (see also Collier 1989; McKay et al. 1997). These school-related registers, as the text example shows, tend to be more like written language, more abstract and less personal, and contain more subject-specific language. Julianna's comment implies she still has difficulties with this more academic language, even though she has no difficulty in expressing herself in more everyday contexts.

This model of language development should not suggest a negative or deficit view of learners like Julianna or of their English skills. Nor should it suggest that the development of school-related language is simply a matter of time and that it will be "picked up" eventually. On the contrary, viewing language development as a process of learning to control an increasing range of registers suggests that while all children are predisposed in a biological sense to learn language, whether or not they actually do, how well they learn to control it, and the range of registers and purposes for which they are able to use it are a matter of the social contexts in which they find themselves.

Second language learners will have experienced a wide range of contexts in which they have learned to use their mother tongue, but a much more restricted range of contexts *in English*. If none of these children's previous language experience is taken into account when the children start school, and if they are expected not only to learn a second language but to learn *in* it as well, it is hardly surprising that without focused English language support they may start to fall behind their peers who are operating in a language they have been familiar with since birth.

While the language and literacy-related demands of the curriculum—the registers of school—are unfamiliar to a greater or lesser extent to all children when they start school, English-speaking children are learning these new concepts and new registers through the medium of their mother tongue, and building on the foundations of their first language, whereas second language learners in an English-medium school are not. Children who are learning through the medium of their first language, and who come to school having already acquired the core grammar of this language and the ability to use it in a range of familiar social situations, have a head start in learning to use the academic registers of school. And as Cummins (1996, 2000) points out, these English-speaking peers do not stand still in their learning and wait for ESL students to "catch up" in the language of instruction. At the same time, we cannot put ESL students' academic development on hold while they are learning the language of instruction. Ultimately, if second language learners are not to be disadvantaged in their long-term learning, and are to have the time and opportunity to learn the subject-specific registers of school, they need access to an ongoing language-focused program across the whole curriculum.

Integrating Language and Content

In countries such as the United States, Canada, the United Kingdom, and Australia, there are increasing numbers of ESL students in school. In the United States, for example, more than 90 percent of recent immigrants come from non-English-speaking countries, and according to the National Center for Education Statistics (1996), there has been a 20 percent increase in the numbers of children who have difficulty with English. Most second language learners spend most of their time in school in mainstream classrooms, even when they receive some English language support from specialist ESL teachers. However, in many countries, this support is rarely available after the learner is past the initial stages of language learning, and the regular classroom teacher must then carry the dual responsibility for the students' subject learning and for their ongoing language development.

Merely exposing ESL learners to content classrooms, however, is not an adequate response: placing students in the mainstream classroom "cannot be assumed to provide optimal language learning opportunities as a matter of course" (Mohan 2001, 108). Teaching programs in all curriculum areas must therefore aim to integrate "language" and "content," so that a second language is developed hand in hand with new curriculum knowledge. This is not a straightforward task. The integration of language, subject content, and thinking skills requires systematic planning and monitoring. And many teachers—and you may be one—have never had the opportunity to complete a specialized ESL program or to prepare for this kind of teaching. This book suggests some of the ways that teachers can respond to the learning and language needs of students learning though their second language, within the context of the regular school curriculum.

A Social View of Teaching and Learning

Two Views of Learning

Since public education began, there have been two major and competing ideologies about the goals of education and the means by which it is to be accomplished (Wells 1999, 2000). The first of these can be described as the "empty vessel" model of teaching and learning, or what Freire (1983) referred to as the "banking" model. Teachers are seen to "deposit" skills or knowledge in the empty memory banks of their students. The teaching-learning relationship is one of transmission and reception—transmission of a body of knowledge by the teacher, and the reception of this knowledge by the students. Language, if it is thought about at all, is seen simply as a conduit or carrier of knowledge.

The second ideology, often referred to as "progressive," appears at one level to be very different. In opposition to the ideology of transmission, the learner is placed at the center of the educational process. Based on the work of Dewey and more recently, Piaget, education is seen not as a matter of receiving information but of intelligent inquiry and thought. In the way that this has been interpreted in some classrooms, the major organizing principle is seen to be the individual child's active construction of knowledge, with the teacher's role being to stage-manage appropriate learning experiences. In this model of learning, action is primary, and a child's language abilities are seen as largely the result of more general and cognitive abilities.

Both orientations have been critiqued from the standpoint of minority students and second language learners (Cummins 1996, 2000). Transmission models tend to work against what is generally accepted as one of the central principles of language learning: namely that using the language in interaction with others is an essential process by which it is learned (see Painter 1985 on mother-tongue development and Swain 1995 on second language development). Transmission pedagogies are also criticized as presenting a curriculum sited solely within the dominant culture, providing little or no opportunity for minority students to express their particular experiences and non-mainstream view of the world. Unfortunately, transmission-based approaches have tended to dominate the education of so-called disadvantaged students, and many compensatory programs have tended to focus on drilling students in low-level language and numeracy skills, effectively structuring ongoing disadvantage into the curriculum of the school (Oakes 1985). Much progressive pedagogy has also been criticized, in particular for its lack of explicit language teaching, which, it has been argued, places a disadvantage on those who are least familiar with the language and assumptions of a middle-class school curriculum (Delpit 1988; Martin 1989; Kalantzis, Cope, Noble, and Poynting 1991). In relation to the teaching of writing, such approaches have been criticized in particular for their focus on the *processes* of language learning, at the expense of focusing sufficiently on the production of written texts. Ultimately, it is argued, the broader social realities of life beyond school require that students will need to be able to control the language that will allow them to participate in the dominant society. This is a powerful argument and is taken up again in Chapter 4.

In reality, both transmission and progressive orientations exist in schools, sometimes together in the same classroom. This is not to be critical of teachers. Rather, it points to the inadequacy of the most common models of learning within which teachers are expected to work. In fact, though very different in the way that they view learning and the role of the teacher, both ideologies have what is essentially an individualistic notion of learning. Whether you view the learner as an empty vessel waiting to be filled with appropriate knowledge, or as an unfolding intellect that will eventually reach its potential given the right environment, both views see the learner as independent and self-contained, and learning as occurring *within* an individual. This book suggests an alternative model, one that foregrounds the collaborative nature of learning and language development *between* individuals, the interrelatedness of the roles of teacher and learner, and the active roles of both in the learning process.

Learning Through Collaboration

The theory of learning on which this book draws is based on the work of Lev Vygotsky (1978, 1986), a Russian psychologist who lived at the beginning of the twentieth century but whose work was not widely translated until the 1960s. Since the 1980s, his work has begun to exert a major influence on Western education in Western Europe,

America, and Australia. Together with the work of other Soviet cognitive researchers—including Luria, Leont'ev, and the literary theorist Bakhtin—and interpretations of this work by scholars and educationists such as Wertsch, Mercer, and Wells, Vygotsky's perspective on human development and learning, broadly termed socio-cultural or socio-historical, offers a radically different perspective from that offered by dominant Western psychological theories. Socio-cultural theory sees human development as intrinsically social rather than individualistic. An individual's development is thus to a significant extent a product, not a prerequisite, of education—the result of his or her social, historical, and cultural experiences. Thus, as suggested earlier in this chapter, while we are all biologically able to acquire language, what language we learn, how adept we are at using it, and the purposes for which we are able to use it are a matter of the social contexts and situations we have been in: in a very real sense, what and how we learn depends very much on the company we keep.

The educational basis for a child's development is encapsulated in what Vygotsky terms the zone of proximal development, by which he refers to the distance or the cognitive gap between what a child can do unaided and what the child can do jointly and in coordination with a more skilled expert. Anyone who has been involved with young children is familiar with this concept. When children are learning to feed or dress themselves, the adult at first has to perform the whole activity. Then the child gradually performs parts of the activity, with the parent still assisting with the more difficult parts. Finally, the child is able to do the whole thing unaided. In other words, successful coordination with a partner—or assisted performance—leads learners to reach beyond what they are able to achieve alone, to participate in new situations and to tackle new tasks, or, in the case of second language learners, to learn new ways of using language.

Vygotsky sees the development of cognition itself also as the result of participation with others in goal-directed activity. A child initially engages in joint thinking with others through the talk that accompanies problem solving and social participation in everyday activity. Imagine, for example, a child doing a jigsaw puzzle with a parent or caregiver. They will probably talk about the shapes of the pieces, what piece might go where, how to match up colors and images, and so on. Vygotsky would argue that this external, social dialogue is gradually internalized to become a resource for individual thinking, or what he refers to as "inner speech." The child's external dialogues with others later become an inner personal resource for the development of thinking and problem solving; eventually the child will do jigsaw puzzles without the need for external dialogue. The child doing the puzzle with the adult is, of course, not only learning how to do that particular puzzle, but becoming familiar with the kind of processes to go through for completing subsequent puzzles. The goal of this kind of learning is to go beyond simply learning items of knowledge to being able to use that knowledge in other contexts—in other words, to learn *how* to think, not simply *what* to think.

As pointed out earlier, second language learners are both learning a new language and learning other things through the medium of the language. If we accept the premise that external dialogue is a major resource for the development of thinking, and that interaction is also integral to language learning, then it follows that we must consider very seriously the nature of the talk in which learners are engaged in the classroom. (This topic is the focus of Chapters 2 and 3 but is a continuing theme throughout the book.)

Let's now look at how these ideas might look in practical terms. Here is an example of a father and mother talking with their son Nigel, who at the time was around fourteen months (taken from Halliday 1975, 112). Nigel had earlier been to the zoo, and while he was looking at a goat, it had attempted to eat a plastic lid that Nigel was holding. The keeper had explained that he shouldn't let the goat eat the lid because it wasn't good for it. As you read this dialogue, look particularly at what the parents are doing, and the effect this has on Nigel's language.

NIGEL:	try eat lid
FATHER:	what tried to eat the lid?
NIGEL:	try eat lid
FATHER:	what tried to eat the lid?
NIGEL:	goat, man said no, goat try eat lid, man said no

Later

NIGEL:	goat try eat lid, man said no
MOTHER:	why did the man say no?
NIGEL:	goat shouldn't eat lid, (*shaking head*) good for it
MOTHER:	the goat shouldn't eat the lid, it's not good for it
NIGEL:	goat try eat lid, man said no, goat shouldn't eat lid, (*shaking head*) good for it.

Notice the kind of scaffolding that the parents provide. Nigel's initial utterance is far from explicit—no one who had not shared the experience with him would be able to understand the significance of what he is saying. First it is not clear what or who Nigel is referring to, and the father's question /what/ shows Nigel what information he needs to provide. Having extended the initial three-word utterance to something significantly more complete, Nigel relates this more extended version to his mother, who pushes the dialogue forward with the question /why/ While Nigel does not take up his mother's use of *shouldn't* (using instead the strategy of indicating a negative by shaking his head), he does provide the reason his mother is seeking (*it's not good for it*), and by the end of these two small conversations he has elaborated on and made more explicit his original short utterance. Most important, what Nigel achieves—the final story he tells—has not simply come from him and his own linguistic resources: this story is a collaborative endeavor, and it has been *jointly* constructed.

This social view of teaching and learning moves us away from the often polarized debate between teacher-centered versus student-centered learning, toward a more unified theory of teaching-and-learning, in which both teachers and students are seen as active participants, and learning is seen as a collaborative endeavor. In line with these collaborative principles, the achievements of second language learners cannot be seen as simply the result of aptitude, background, or individual motivation, but are also dependent on the social and linguistic frameworks within which their learning takes place: language learning is a socially embedded process, not simply a psychologically driven process. Thus what teachers choose to do in classrooms, and in particular the kinds of support they provide, is of crucial importance in the educational success of their students. It is to the nature of this support or *scaffolding* that we now turn.

Scaffolding

The term *scaffolding* was first used by Wood, Bruner, and Ross (1976) in their examination of parent-child talk in the early years. It is a useful metaphor that we will use throughout the book. Scaffolding—in its more usual sense—is a temporary structure that is often put up in the process of constructing a building. As each bit of the new building is finished, the scaffolding is taken down. The scaffolding is temporary, but essential for the successful construction of the building. Bruner (1978) describes scaffolding in the metaphorical sense in which we are using it here, as "the steps taken to reduce the degrees of freedom in carrying out some tasks so that the child can concentrate on the difficult skill she is in the process of acquiring" (19). In the classroom it portrays the "temporary, but essential, nature of the mentor's assistance" in supporting learners to carry out tasks successfully (Maybin, Mercer, and Stierer 1992, 186). *Scaffolding,* however, is not simply another word for *help.* It is a special kind of help that assists learners to move toward new skills, concepts, or levels of understanding. Scaffolding is thus the temporary assistance by which a teacher helps a learner know how to do something, so that the learner will later be able to complete a similar task alone. It is future-oriented: as Vygotsky has said, what a child can do with support today, she or he can do alone tomorrow.

It can be argued that it is only *when* teacher support—or scaffolding—is needed that learning will take place, since the learner is then likely to be working within his or her zone of proximal development; Vygotsky (1978) suggests that the only "good" learning is learning that is ahead of actual development. While this idea does not ignore the notion that teaching experiences should not be completely beyond the capacity of the learner, it does challenge the notion of learner "readiness" by suggesting that it is the teacher who is largely responsible for initiating each new step of learning, building on what a learner is currently able to do alone. It challenges teachers to maintain high expectations of all students, but to provide adequate scaffolding for tasks to be completed successfully. In terms of ESL students, it suggests a somewhat different orientation to learning tasks than has often been the case in the past. Rather than simplifying the *task* (and ultimately risking a reductionist curriculum), we should instead reflect on the nature of the *scaffolding* that is being provided for learners to carry out that task. As far as possible, learners need to be engaged with authentic and cognitively challenging learning tasks; it is the nature of the support—support that is responsive to the particular demands made on children learning through the medium of a second language—that is critical for success.

This book offers many suggestions for scaffolding learning for second language learners in the regular classroom. However, it is worth remembering that the presence of ESL children in a school, while posing a challenge for many mainstream teachers, can also be at the same time a catalyst for the kind of language-focused curriculum that will be of benefit to all children. As a result of poverty or social background or nonstandard dialect, native speakers of English may also have difficulty with the specialized registers of curriculum subjects. Recognizing that the language of these subjects cannot be taken for granted but has to be taught, finding stimulating and effective ways to do so, and critically examining how language is currently being used in one's own classroom will assist not only second language learners but also many of their monolingual-English peers.

What This Book Is About

Cummins (2000) suggests four key areas that schools should address in order to be inclusive of minority students: (1) community and parent participation; (2) cultural and linguistic incorporation; (3) assessment; and (4) pedagogy. In a large United States study, "School Effectiveness for Language Minority Students," Thomas and Collier (1999) found three key predictors of academic success to be more important than any other set of variables, such as socioeconomic status or gender. The first predictor was English language support through subject areas combined with support in the first language. The second was the use of current approaches to teaching the curriculum through two languages. The third was the socio-cultural climate of the school itself: where the school curriculum was inclusive of ESL students and of their language and cultural background, and where the teachers' expectations of their students were high, ESL student achievement was high.

It is outside the scope of this book to be inclusive of all these areas. Its major focus is on pedagogy, and the integrated teaching of English as a Second Language across the curriculum. However, the importance of the areas identified by Cummins and by Thomas and Collier should be noted since good English teaching alone is an insufficient response to the teaching of minority groups. The following chapters should therefore be read against this broader perspective.

The book takes the view that assessment is integral to pedagogy, and is a vital source of information about students' language-learning needs. It suggests that one of the most important factors influencing learning is what the student already knows. Chapter 7 focuses on language learning across the curriculum. It includes examples of how teachers can use day-to-day teaching and learning activities to assess students' comprehension and use of language, and how this information can feed into future programming. In this way, assessment plays an "advocacy" role (Cummins 1996); it informs the planning of future teaching and learning tasks and is aimed at supporting students' academic and linguistic development.

A further perspective is that second language development involves a continuing process of meaning making. While the "formal" aspects of language—grammatical accuracy, phonics knowledge, and spelling—cannot (and should not) be ignored, the assumption in this book is that these aspects of language learning are best focused on in the context of authentic meaning making and curriculum learning, within a classroom in which dialogue between learners is valued. In other words, learning *about* language is most meaningful when it occurs in the context of actual language use.

The following five chapters each focus specifically on the teaching of speaking, writing, reading, or listening, in the context of a range of school subjects. However, while the major focus of each chapter is on one skill in particular, the teaching activities they discuss usually involve the integration of all four skills: speaking, listening, reading, and writing. Thus it is not suggested that these skills should be *taught* discretely: as the examples illustrate, this book favors an integrative and across-the-curriculum approach. They have been separated in these chapters in order to allow each to be discussed fully, and because, in the classroom, even though a particular activity might be integrated with other skills, it is sometimes important for the teacher to focus on only one of them. Speaking, and even more so, listening, have too often been the poor relations to reading and writing and sometimes not received the attention they deserve.

The next two chapters focus on the development of spoken language. Chapter 2 discusses the development of spoken language both as a tool for learning and as a bridge into literacy. It suggests ways in which communicative approaches can be built into the curriculum, and gives examples of the kind of talk that is likely to enable language development. Chapter 3 focuses on teacher-student talk, and shows how teachers can build on the continuum introduced briefly in this chapter. Chapter 4 discusses the teaching of writing. It describes the major linguistic features of a range of writing forms common in primary schools, and suggests a teaching model by which specific forms of writing—text types or genres—can be developed across the curriculum. Chapter 5 focuses on the teaching of reading and includes examples of a range of activities that help students access the meaning of the text and model what effective readers do when they read. Chapter 6 focuses on listening and discusses what kinds of listening demands are made on listeners in different contexts. It also describes a range of activities aimed at improving children's listening skills. Chapter 7 draws together the theories and practical activities of the previous chapters. It illustrates how the regular curriculum can be exploited for the purposes of language teaching, and how an ESL-aware content curriculum can be related both to the identified language needs of the students and to the language demands of the subject area. The final section of the book is a glossary of all the teaching and learning activities mentioned in earlier chapters. It describes and gives extra information about how to use them. Activities that are described in the glossary are written in bold type in the text.

In Summary

This chapter has introduced the notion of language in context: language varies according to the contexts in which it occurs. Drawing on the work of Halliday, we have argued that language learning is therefore not a linear process, but involves learners in developing language in an increasing range of contexts. For ESL students, this requires English language support across the whole curriculum. We have also suggested that learning is essentially collaborative and social, and that both teacher and students are partners in this collaborative learning. For the teacher, this means building on what students already know, and providing scaffolding that is responsive to the needs of ESL students for the language and tasks they are not yet able to do alone.

Second language learners are not a homogenous group, but are as varied in terms of their background, experiences, language, expectations, values, culture, and socioeconomic status as any other group of students. More important, they can no longer be thought of as a group apart from the mainstream—in today's culturally and linguistically diverse classrooms, they *are* the mainstream. As Clegg (1996) points out:

> We should see ESL learners as full members of the school community, who have specific learning needs, rather than as a separate group who must prove themselves linguistically before they can claim their full entitlement. (5)

The following chapters illustrate how subject learning can also be language learning, and suggest some of the ways in which teachers can scaffold learning and language so that ESL learners are seen "as full members of the school community."

Suggestions for Further Reading

CUMMINS, J. 1996. "The Deep Structure of Educational Reform." Chapter 6 in *Negotiating Identities: Education for Empowerment in a Diverse Society*, ed. J. Cummins. Ontario, CA: California Association for Bilingual Education.

CUMMINS, J. 2000. "Language Proficiency in Academic Contexts." Chapter 3 in *Language, Power and Pedagogy: Bilingual Children in the Crossfire*, ed. J. Cummins. Clevedon, UK: Multilingual Matters.

DELPIT, L. 1988. "The Silenced Dialogue: Power and Pedagogy in Educating Other People's Children." *Harvard Educational Review* 58 (3): 280–98.

MERCER, N. 1994. "Neo-Vygotskian Theory and Classroom Education." In *Language, Literacy and Learning in Educational Practice*, ed. B. Stierer and J. Maybin. Clevedon, UK: Multilingual Matters.

MOHAN, B. 2001. "The Second Language as a Medium of Learning." In *English as a Second Language in the Mainstream: Teaching, Learning and Identity*, ed. B. Mohan, C. Leung, and C. Davison. London: Longman.

2

Classroom Talk
Creating Contexts for Language Learning

Language is our cultural tool—we use it to share experience and so to collectively, jointly, make sense of it . . . Language is therefore not just a means by which individuals can formulate ideas and communicate them, it is also a means for people to think and learn together.
Neil Mercer, *The Guided Construction of Knowledge*

The Role of Talk in Learning

In this chapter and the next we will explore one of the most fundamental things that goes on in all classrooms—talk. In most classrooms, it is probably true to say that someone is talking for most of the time; time spent on talking probably accounts for the bulk of time students and teachers spend in school. But compared to the research that has gone on about the teaching of reading and writing, and the time that has been put into literacy programs, curriculum development, and syllabus design, talk must be seen as very much the poor relation to the teaching of the written mode. Yet, as we discussed in Chapter 1, the development of the spoken forms of language are essential for second language learners as a bridge to the more academic language associated with learning in school, and with the development of literacy.

Vygotskian theory also points to the significance of interaction in learning and, as we saw in Chapter 1, views dialogue as constructing the resources for thinking. The quality of the dialogues that children are engaged in must therefore be looked at critically. They need to stimulate "thinking aloud," or what Wegerif and Mercer (1996) refer to as "exploratory talk." This is the kind of talk that allows learners to explore and clarify concepts or to try out a line of thought, through questioning, hypothesizing, making logical deductions, and responding to others' ideas. But at the same time, classroom tasks must also provide the conditions that will foster second language development.

In this chapter, we first discuss how children engaged in collaborative group work learn language and learn through language, and discuss some of the principles for setting up successful group tasks. Later we look at how a teacher working with a whole class can also, through his or her interactions with students, provide opportunities for language development and learning.

We have already seen in Chapter 1 the important role interaction plays in the process of children learning their first language. The importance of talk more generally in learning has long been recognized (see for example Barnes 1976; Bruner 1978). More recently, largely influenced by the work of Vygotsky, the social and cultural basis for learning has been recognized (Mercer 1995, 2000; Wells 2000). As we have seen, this perspective puts interaction at the heart of the learning process. The classroom is viewed as a place where understanding and knowledge are jointly constructed between teachers and students, and where learners are guided or "apprenticed" into the broader understandings and language of the curriculum and the particular subject discipline. The notion of apprenticeship into a culture is particularly relevant in an ESL school context, where, in order to participate in society, students must learn to control the dominant genres and ways of thinking through which that culture is constructed (Delpit 1988; Kalantzis, Cope, Noble, and Poynting 1991).

Research that has come out of second language acquisition studies also suggests that interaction is a significant factor in language development (see, for example, Ellis 1994; Swain 1995; van Lier 1996). Of particular importance are the kinds of interactions that occur as speakers clarify their intended meaning, such as when speakers have an opportunity to negotiate and reword what they are trying to say (Pica, Young, and Doughty 1987; Pica 1994). Research into French immersion programs, French-speaking schools that are designed for English-speaking students and that aim to develop bilingual skills, has suggested that language "output" by the student—that is, the language produced by the learners themselves—is critical for language development (Allen, Swain, Harley, and Cummins 1990; Swain 1995). This research found that while students developed considerable fluency in their second language (French), many did not develop native-like proficiency or grammatical accuracy, despite hearing a great deal of French and being in a communicatively oriented classroom where French was used for learning subject content. Swain suggests that what was missing in these classrooms was sufficient opportunity for students to produce extended stretches of French themselves. She argues that actually producing language encourages learners to process the language more deeply than is required when they simply listen, and tends to stretch or push learner language in a way that listening alone does not. (If you have struggled to make yourself understood in another language, you will recognize that it is often at these moments of struggle that real steps in learning are achieved.)

Swain also argues that when the context requires learners to focus on the ways they are expressing themselves, they are pushed to produce more comprehensible, coherent, and grammatically improved discourse. The classroom implication for this is not that language "form" per se should become a major teaching focus, but that it is important, at times, for learners to have opportunities to use stretches of discourse in contexts where there is a press on their linguistic resources, and where, for the benefit of their listeners, they must focus not only on what they wish to say but on how they are saying it. The activities suggested in this chapter set up contexts where this is likely to occur.

Classroom Talk and ESL Learners

One clear teaching implication of studies into second language acquisition is that the degree of facility of second language learning in a classroom depends largely on how classroom discourse is constructed. Think for a moment about the patterns of interaction that typify many classrooms. There is a particular kind of three-part exchange between teacher and student that is very familiar to all teachers (and to their students) and that a number of researchers have described as being the dominant interactional pattern in classrooms (Sinclair and Coulthard 1975; Mehan 1979; Edwards and Mercer 1987). In this pattern of interaction, the teacher first asks a question (almost certainly one to which he or she knows the answer); the student responds, often with a single word or short answer; and then the teacher responds by evaluating the answer. Such interactions are sometimes referred to as IRF (Initiation, Response, Feedback) or IRE (Initiation, Response, Evaluation). Here are two examples:

- *Initiation*   TEACHER: What season comes after fall?
  Response   STUDENT: Winter.
  Feedback   TEACHER: Good girl.

- *Initiation*   TEACHER: Now everyone, who can tell me what these are called?
  Response   STUDENT 1:   A compass?
  Feedback   TEACHER: Not quite, nearly right . . .
  Response   STUDENT 2:   A pair of compasses.
  Feedback   TEACHER: Right, good!
  Initiation   TEACHER: And who knows what we can use them for?
  Response   STUDENT 3:   Making circles?
  Feedback   TEACHER: Right, we can draw circles with them

The IRF pattern is based on what has become known as a "display" question, a question that is primarily designed for students to display their learning. It is a common pattern in traditional classrooms, particularly where the teacher sees his or her role primarily as transmitting a body of information. Of course, such interaction patterns are sometimes very useful, such as when the teacher's questions serve to provide a framework for a logical thought process, such as talking students through a math problem. So it would be foolish to suggest that teachers should avoid all such interactions altogether or that whole-class work is inappropriate. On the contrary, the second part of this chapter illustrates how teacher-student interactions, with a little modification to the pattern just shown, can be very effective in supporting language development.

However, if we look at the examples just shown, it's easy to see that what they *don't* fulfil is the need for students to produce "comprehensible output." When teacher initiations lead only to single-word or single-clause responses, there is little opportunity for the learner's language to be stretched, for students to focus on how they are saying something, or for giving them practice in using the language for themselves. The teacher in fact says far more than the students do! It is this kind of interaction that prompted Edwards and Mercer (1987) to refer to the "two thirds" rule when they suggested, somewhat humorously but probably very accurately, that in most classrooms someone is talking for most of the time, for most of the time it is the teacher, and for most of the time the teacher is either lecturing or asking questions.

Teacher-student talk of this kind may therefore actually deprive learners of just those interactional features and conditions that research suggests are enabling factors in second language learning. A classroom program that is supportive of second language learning must therefore create opportunities for more varied and dialogic interactional patterns to occur.

Group Work and Second Language Learning

As the prior discussion suggests, where language development is a major objective of a teaching program, there must be alternatives to IRF interactional patterns, and these need to be deliberately planned and set up. One of the ways in which teachers can do this is through the use of group work. Group work has a number of advantages for language learning.

When group work is set up effectively (and we will look at what this involves later in this chapter), it has important advantages over whole-class work for second language learning. McGroarty (1993) suggests that it offers benefits to second language learners in three ways that are important for language learning:

1. Learners hear more language, a greater variety of language, and have more language directed toward them: group-work situations increase the *input* to the learner.
2. Learners *interact* more with other speakers, and therefore their *output* is also increased. They tend to take more turns, and in the absence of the teacher, have more responsibility for clarifying their own meanings. In other words, it is the learners themselves who are doing the language learning work.
3. What learners hear and what they learn is *contextualized*: language is heard and used in an appropriate context and used meaningfully for a particular purpose.

In addition:

- There is likely to be considerable *message redundancy*—that is, similar ideas will be expressed in a variety of different ways. Asking questions, exchanging information, and solving problems all provide a context where words are repeated, ideas are rephrased, problems are restated, and meanings are refined. This redundancy supports comprehension, because it gives learners several opportunities to hear a similar idea expressed in a number of ways.

- The need to get information or clarify meaning increases the opportunities for learners to ask questions that genuinely seek new information, and thus there is further input and practice in genuine communication. (Compare this with whole-class contexts where it is much more usual for the teacher to ask the questions, and where students are often required to answer only for the purposes of showing what they know.)
- Finally, we should not forget that group work may have positive affective consequences: learners who are not confident in English often feel more comfortable working with peers than being expected to perform in a whole-class situation.

Here is an example that illustrates how children working together can collaboratively do more than they can individually, and demonstrates again the collaborative nature of learning discussed in Chapter 1. In this classroom, different groups of children had each done a different experiment, all of which were designed to show the effects of magnetic repulsion. The teacher had told all the children they would report to the rest of the class about what happened, and what they had learned from doing their particular experiment. This informal reporting was a regular occurrence in the classroom, and, as we will see in the next chapter, it was a time when children could develop common understandings and clarify new learning, and when new language and developing concepts could be "recycled" or reviewed.

Before the reporting session began, the teacher explained to the students that they needed to make what they said clear and comprehensible to their listeners, and they needed to remember that the rest of the class did not know what other groups had done. She explained that their language needed to be very clear and precise so that everyone could understand what happened. She instructed the students to help the other children to "try to get a picture in their mind of what you did." At the beginning of the reporting lesson, the children were given a few minutes to think about what they would tell their peers.

In the group we focus on here, all the children but Emily, who was a fluent bilingual in Chinese and English, were identified as having ESL needs, and Milad and Maroun were in the early stages of learning English. For their experiment, they were asked to use a small polystyrene block into which a number of Popsicle sticks (referred to as paddle pop sticks) had been inserted to form a cradle to hold a bar magnet in place. The group was asked to test the effect of a second bar magnet when it was placed above the first, and then to reverse the position of the second magnet. They recorded their results. (Depending on the relative position of the poles, the magnets either attracted or repelled. When repulsion occurred, the top magnet appeared to be floating above the bottom magnet.) In the dialogue that follows, they are planning how they will report back to the class about this science experiment.

In the examples of the classroom talk in this book, a dot represents approximately a one-second pause. Traditional punctuation is not used, since the excerpts are transcriptions of *spoken* language.

EMILY: we have to talk about what we did last time and what were the results . . .

MILAD: we got em . . . we got a . thing like . . . this . . . pu- we got paddle pop sticks and we got

MAROUN: we put them in a pot

MILAD: and have to try and put

GINA: wasn't in a pot . . . it's like a foam . . .

MILAD: a foam

EMILY: a block of foam

GINA: and we put it

EMILY: we put paddle pops around it, the foam, and then we put the magnet in it

GINA: and then we got

EMILY: and then we got another magnet and put it on top, and it wasn't touching the other magnet . .

MAROUN: when we . . . when we turned it the other way . . . it didn't stick on because . . . because

GINA: because?

MAROUN: because em . . . it was on a different . . . side

MILAD: Emily your go

EMILY: OK. last week we . . . we . . . did an experiment . . . we had a em a block of foam and we um . . . stuck paddle pop sticks in it and we put . . . a magnet, a bar of magnet . . . into the em cradle that we made with the paddle pop sticks. Then we put another magnet on top and the result of this was . . . the magnet that we put on top of the cradled magnet did not stick to the other magnet.

GINA: then when we turned it around. When we turned the other magnet around it . . .

MAROUN: stuck

MILAD: it stuck together because

MAROUN: and it stuck together because it was

EMILY: it was on a different side

GINA: it was on a different side and the other one's and

EMILY: and the poles are different

GINA: and the poles are different

MILAD: and em when . . . we put on the first side it stuck together . . .

GINA: because em it was on different sides, because we put it on the on the thin side and it didn't and we didn't . . it didn't stick . .

MAROUN: because the flat side is stronger than the thin side?

EMILY: no, because the poles are different

MILAD: because the poles are different, alright?

What can we learn from this example? It is clear that a lot is being learned in this group talk, both about science and about how to talk about it. All the children participate in *jointly* constructing this discourse. For example, the term *block of foam* is finally reached through a progressive clarification of an appropriate way to name it, and this is built up by three speakers: *a pot, not a pot, a foam,* (repeated), *a block of foam.* Students complete each other's remarks and prompt each other to continue. The main scientific understanding of the experiment is built up across seven turns that together construct the statement: *when we turned the other magnet around it stuck together because it was on a different side and the poles are different.* Through the process of joint construction, the wording is gradually refined toward more explicit and written-like language, and scientific understandings are reworked and modified (note that *different sides* becomes *different poles*). Individual students are scaffolded by the contributions of the group as a whole.

And so we can see that this kind of collective scaffolding is at times as useful as that provided by the teacher. Although no student, except for Emily, possesses the ability to construct this report alone, the students are able *collectively* to reach an appropriate wording. Note, however, that this talk is not simply a functionally "empty" language exercise, but the result of a real and shared purpose for the students, who knew that one of them would be expected to share his or her learning with the class. Gina, who was chosen by the teacher for this task, explained her group's experiment like this:

> We put paddle pop sticks around the block of foam . . . and then . . . we got a magnet and put it in . . . and we got another magnet and put it on top but it wasn't touching the other magnet and then . when we turned it around it attach together, the two magnets, when we put it on the side they attach . because . . because the poles are different.

It seems unlikely that she would have been able to speak as fluently as this without the initial talk in a group. Notice that what she says here is beginning to sound more like "written" language. As the next chapter will also suggest, oral reporting to others is a useful bridge to writing.

Making Group Work Effective

How then should group work be organized if it is to be effective? What follows are some important principles for group work that has, as part of its aim, the development of language. You may find it useful to use these as a checklist when you are planning or carrying out group- or pair-work activities.

Clear and Explicit Instructions Are Provided

This may seem very obvious, yet it is often at the setting-up stage that even a well-designed task can go wrong. As you may have observed in your own teaching, one of the hardest listening tasks for ESL learners is to understand and remember a string of instructions. While a single instruction may cause no problems, instructions that involve a number of sequenced steps are often far more difficult. Try to put into practice the notion of "message redundancy" discussed earlier, by giving the same instructions in several ways. For example, after you have told children what they are to do, ask someone to retell what you said to the rest of the class, or ask individual children to tell you each step in turn. Write it up on the board as they say it. Written instructions on cards are also useful and will help keep children on task. And remember that it is often better to demonstrate a game or activity with a student as your partner than to give an explanation in words. In some tasks, and particularly with beginners, the language of the explanation is often more complex than the language involved in the task itself!

Here is an example of a teacher giving instructions to a group of ESL children who are about to carry out the science experiment described earlier. First, she read from written instructions:

> Place a bar magnet into the cradle made by the paddle pop sticks. Place a second bar magnet on top. Observe and record what happens. Repeat, alternating the poles. Observe and record what happens.

Then she explained the instructions, providing scaffolding for the children (see Figure 2–1). The right-hand column comments on what the teacher was doing physically and on the language she used.

The teacher then went on to discuss what it means to *observe*, and the ways in which students could record what occurred. She also gave a copy of the instructions to the group before they began the experiment.

The commentary column gives a good idea of how this teacher made sure the instructions were comprehensible to her students. Notice how she introduced the use of more formal terms (such as *place* and *alternate*) alongside more usual and familiar terms (*put* and *change*) so that through this parallelism children could see the equivalencies in meaning. At the same time, she demonstrated the meaning of what she was saying by physically handling the materials with which the children would be working. Finally, the children had a set of written instructions to which they could later refer (and that also modeled a more formal example of language use). Note that the teacher was not simply giving the children a set of *simplified* instructions. On the contrary, the written instructions were fairly typical of more formal written language and were

Teacher's words	Commentary
You have to place a magnet, put a magnet, into the cradle, and place another magnet on top of the cradled magnet	*teacher refers to the written instructions, introduces less well-known word* place *alongside more familiar word* put.
So you've got one magnet in here	*pointing*
then you have to put another magnet on top, right?	*holding the second magnet, indicating where it must be placed but not actually placing it*
. then you have to alt-ern-ate the magnets.	alternate *is said slowly and with emphasis*
It says "alternating the poles" . . . changing the poles.	*models the more formal word (*alternate*) but uses this along with a familiar "everyday" word (*change*); also holds the second magnet and indicates how the magnet should be turned*
so if you put it facing like this . . . you've got it one way like this,	*demonstrating*
then you change the poles around	*indicating the movement by turning the second magnet in the air but not placing it*
change it to the other side, alternate the poles.	*switches between more and less formal terms*
So you're trying it each way	*summarizing what the children should do.*

Figure 2–1. *Scaffolding Instructions*

appropriate for the age level of the children. At the same time, the teacher was building bridges into this written text so that the learners were given access to new and more formal language. She was amplifying, not simplifying, the language.

Talk Is Necessary for the Task

A group task should *require*, not simply *encourage*, talk. Let's imagine that you are working with the topic of insects. If you ask groups of children simply to "talk about" a picture of insects, there is no real reason or need for the picture to be discussed, and probably not all children will join in. In this case talk is invited, even encouraged, but it is not *required*, since there is no authentic purpose for using it. However, if you give a pair of children two similar pictures of insects that differ in some details (see Figure

FIGURE 2–2. *Find the Difference*

2–2), and ask them to find the differences between them (without showing each other their pictures), this would *require* talk: without it, the task cannot be carried out. They each need to describe their pictures aloud in order to determine what is different. This particular kind of pair activity is called a **Find the Difference** Game.

   The best pedagogic tasks involve some kind of *information gap*—that is, a situation whereby different members within a group, or individuals in a pair, hold different or incomplete information, so that the only way that the task can be completed is for this information to be shared. The Find the Difference Game in Figure 2–2 illustrates this principle. Pair activities like this are often called "barrier games," referring to the fact that partners do not *show* each other their information.

It is possible to use the information gap principle with a whole class. In the science classroom we have been discussing, the teacher had set up five different experiments, all designed to develop students' understanding of the concepts of magnetic attraction and repulsion. The teacher's original plan was for all groups of students to do each of these experiments over the course of a couple of weeks, and then to report to the whole class about what they had learned. On reflection the teacher decided against this, since this would have resulted in students talking about what was already familiar to the rest of the class (given that they would all have done the same things). Instead, the teacher revised her plan and decided that each group would do a different experiment, so that when the time came for reporting what they had learned, each group would be talking about something unknown to their audience; they would be the "experts" in what they had done, and there would be a context for genuine information sharing. Talking about something that the rest of the class hasn't experienced themselves also requires students to be very explicit about what they have learned, and to focus on making what they say comprehensible to the rest of the class.

Organizing the class into **expert and home groups** also fulfills the principle of creating an information gap with a whole class. The basic idea here is that different groups of learners become "experts" in a particular aspect of a topic. For example, in a topic about insects, each group may choose to research a particular insect under certain whole-class headings, such as *description, habitat, food, life cycle,* and *interesting facts.* After each group has become an expert in one particular insect, the students go into new groups, so that one person from each expert group is in each new group. Then each person shares his or her "expert" knowledge with the other group members.

In this way, each individual becomes an expert in the home group and now has the responsibility of sharing what he or she knows, while the nonexperts make notes. In this way all information is shared, and the resulting notes may become the basis for a piece of writing. Expert and home groups are described more fully in the Glossary, and in Chapter 4.

There Is a Clear Outcome for the Group Work

In well-designed activities, something *happens* as a result of the language being used. There will be an outcome, a result, such as the solving of a problem, or the sharing of information. Learners should be clear about what this outcome should be. For example, in the **Find the Difference** Game, they should know the number of differences they are looking for, and know that they must name them. In the expert/home group activity, the outcome will be that all children will have a set of written notes based on what others have said and on their own research. It's important to make the outcome of the task explicit to students when you are setting it up, so that they understand the purpose of what they are doing and can see how it fits into a bigger picture.

The Task Is Cognitively Appropriate to the Learners

Ideally, the task should be at an appropriate level of cognitive challenge for the age of the learners. This is not always easy to achieve, since with older learners who are very new to English, tasks need to be cognitively demanding at the same time as having relatively low English language demands. However, in general, when tasks are integrated into a curriculum area, it is more likely that thinking is involved. Older learners are also likely to have some literacy skills, and it may be that part of the task can draw on first language resources. For example, students may initially discuss, read, or write in their first language. Try to involve beginners in tasks that are less dependent on language, such as experiential science or mathematics activities, where they will be able to experience success and participate more easily. And remember that such tasks provide an essential respite from the intense demands of continuously operating in an unfamiliar language.

The Task Is Integrated with a Broader Curriculum Topic

We have seen in Chapter 1 how a functional view of language relates language to the context in which it is used. We do not first "learn" language and then later "use" it. Second language learners do not in any case have the time to study English as a "subject" before they use it to learn other things: they must begin to use it as a medium for learning as soon as they enter school, simultaneously developing their second language hand-in-hand with curriculum knowledge. As Mohan (2001) points out, we cannot place ESL students' academic development on hold while they are learning English. And so as far as possible, language learning tasks should be integrated with learning across the curriculum. Language tasks and exercises that are simply an "add-on" to the curriculum not only work against this, but are a frustrating experience for the teacher who then has to find time for such extra work. In Chapter 7 we will look in more detail at how program planning can incorporate both language and content objectives. Here I will note only that one of the advantages of situating language teaching within a curriculum area is that the language and conceptual content will be more familiar to students, and the language practice gained in the activity itself can help to introduce or recycle the concepts, grammar, or vocabulary associated with particular curriculum knowledge. All the activities and tasks listed in the Glossary can be situated within a range of subject areas, and they can be integrated with the particular topic being studied.

All Children in the Group Are Involved

As a teacher, you will no doubt have had students who don't participate in group work, perhaps because they don't like working in this way, feel insecure about their contribution, are dominated by others in the group, or simply prefer to let others do the work. There are two ways in which you can help ensure that all children are involved.

First, the overall organizational structure can be such that it requires the participation of all group members. Expert/home groupings require that all members carry out their responsibilities, or otherwise the home group will not have all the information it needs. And the peer group is very good at making sure this work gets done! As I overheard one learner insist to another, when a home group was sharing information on insects, "Go on, you tell us, *you're* the butterfly!" Students are urged to take responsibility because the group wants them to, not just because the teacher expects them to. In this way, group work serves as an effective prompt for learning and helps students develop a sense of personal worth and responsibility.

Second, until children are used to working in groups, members of the group should each have a role to play. These can include a timekeeper, a recorder, a reporter, someone who keeps the group on task, someone who ensures everyone has an opportunity to contribute, and so on. Not only does this give a special responsibility to all the members of the group, but it also helps ensure that the group work runs effectively.

Students Have Enough Time to Complete Tasks

The question of time is a very important one: too much, and children are likely to waste it; not enough, and they are unlikely to learn effectively or be able to engage in the activity as fully as they could. Second language students are likely to take longer to complete language-based tasks, since they need longer to process what they hear and to respond to language that is directed to them. I have found that inexperienced teachers will often design a wonderful set of tasks but aim to do too much in one lesson, so that children are no sooner into one task than another one is begun. Well-designed tasks are worth exploiting. Don't underestimate the time it takes to give clear instructions, for the task to be completed, and for a summing up of what students have done or learned. Each of these processes involve language and are an opportunity to model, recycle, and revise it. They can be as much a part of the learning as the task itself or the end product.

Students Know How to Work in Groups

Working in groups is a learned skill—even some adults are not good at it! If learners are unable to work collaboratively, even the best-designed teaching activities are unlikely to be successful. Effective participation implies the taking of initiative, and that is only possible when students understand and subscribe to the "rules" of classroom behavior. While most classrooms have some agreed-upon rules for behavior, group work is often based on "unwritten" and assumed knowledge about how to work together. Making such knowledge explicit is helpful for all children, but especially for those less familiar with the learning culture and norms of the school.

Here is an example of one teacher talking with her students about working collaboratively in a group. As a conclusion to work on magnets, the children are about to design a game based on the properties of magnets. The teacher is talking with the children about what makes group work a success.

TEACHER: you're going to come up with *one* game . . OK . . . so you have to do a lot of negotiating, because you're all going to have lots of good ideas . . but if . . . is it going to be like this . . . get into the group . . . and say, "I know what we're doing, me me me, I've decided?" is that how we work in groups?

STUDENTS: no.

TEACHER: what sorts of things can we remember? Simon?

SIMON: em . . . share your ideas?

TEACHER: good take turns share your ideas because four people's ideas or three people's ideas have to be better than one person's ideas, don't they? we'll get a lot more . . Fabiola?

FABIOLA: communicate with your group.

TEACHER: how do you *communicate* with your group . . . that's very true, but how do you do it?

FABIOLA: like instead of . . . em when you start with your group you don't em shout, and don't . . . "I know what we should do and this is what we can do . . " and if someone want to talk it over say "no, *this* is what we're going to do."

TEACHER: OK . . so it's a lot of . . . first of all, turn taking, and quiet group-work voices, and maybe sharing your ideas . . certainly . "oh, an idea I have" or "one idea I have," or "a suggestion that I have" . . put it forward as a suggestion or an idea . . people will be much more willing to listen to it than if you say . . "this is what we're going to do . . so be careful with the sort of group-work language that you use"

GINA: Miss how about if like . . . you have four people in your group and one want [sic] to do something and another one want to do something else and they all want to do different things?

TEACHER: they've all got different ideas? good. good question . . does anyone have any suggestions for Gina? if you get into your group and everyone says "well this is my idea," "this is my idea" "this is my idea," "this is my idea" . . and no one wants to . . . move from their idea?

[Lots of students indicate they have ideas]

TEACHER: what could be some strategies? Duncan.

DUNCAN: em, you could put them all together . . . like . . . like make them one.

FABIOLA: make up into one game

TEACHER: OK so maybe try to combine the ideas to make up one game, that could be one thing . . what if they don't go together, though? what if the ideas are very very different? how could you work with it then Anna?

ANNA: em you could em find a piece of paper and write it and scrunch up and put it into a hat

TEACHER: OK choose it . . . maybe say "Alright, we can't decide . . . so that's the most fair way to do it . ." that could be one way . . that's another suggestion . yes Charbel?

CHARBEL: do an arm wrestle? [*laughing*]

TEACHER: oh probably not the most appropriate way . certainly an idea. [*laughing*] yes . we might get ourselves into real trouble though . . . thank you, I don't think Mr. W. [*the principal*] would be too impressed if he walked in and saw us arm wrestling over what we decide to do . he probably wouldn't think that was appropriate group-work behavior . [*laughing*] Robert?

"*Do an arm wrestle?*"

ROBERT: miss if you can't think of one you can em . . . you can you can . . . play it? and see which one's a good one.

TEACHER: OK good suggestion . . yes, Andre?

ANDRE: Oh Miss like . . . you're going to vote for which one is the most fun

TEACHER: that's a good idea . maybe you could say you can't vote for your own but you can vote for one of the others . sometimes though it's just . . . not being stubborn . . . you know . thinking . really trying to step back and think "well, it doesn't matter whose idea it is, but what would be the best idea for the task that we're trying to complete?"

This kind of talk makes explicit to children some of the ways they will be expected to work. But perhaps even more important is the fact that the "rules" are collaboratively built up, with the children's contributions being valued by the teacher and expanded on. In this process, the teacher also provides models of what (and what not!) to say. The interpersonal language involved in working collaboratively, such as knowing how to express agreement and disagreement, knowing how to offer an opinion, knowing how to build on a suggestion, or knowing how to request something politely or give advice, may not be known in English by some students. Remember that the language of the classroom is not simply the language of the content being studied, but includes these interpersonal aspects of learning too. I have sometimes heard teachers complaining that their ESL students are impolite or abrupt, yet the reason is often simply that the students do not have access to this kind of language *in English*, or that it has never been made salient or explicit to them.

So building this into your teaching, at those times when it is most relevant, is an important part of the ESL program. And remember that one of the most simple and effective ways for improving group work is to talk with the children about what the teacher shown here referred to as "quiet group-work voices"! Encourage children to speak as quietly as possible, so as to avoid the situation all too familiar to teachers, when noise levels steadily increase as everyone seeks to make themselves heard above the others.

Remember that for ESL learners, a noisy environment makes comprehension that much harder.

Some Suggestions for Group and Pair Activities Across the Curriculum

Here are some examples of types of activities to use with groups. They can all be adapted for a range of levels and subject areas.

✴ *Picture Sequencing*

For this activity, you will need a set of picture cards that tell a simple and predictable story or illustrate a predictable sequence (see Figure 2–3). Give each student in the group one card (there should be the same number of students as there are picture cards). Tell the students not to show the others in their group their card. Each student describes their card (it doesn't matter who starts), and when they have all finished

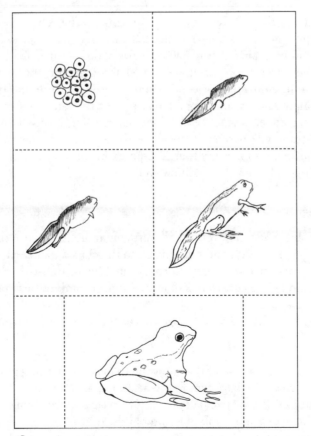

FIGURE 2–3. *Picture Sequencing*

describing the cards, the group decides on the basis of the descriptions which card should come first, which second, and so on. On the basis of the order decided, the students put down their cards in sequence. For younger students and those very new to English, make sure that cards are placed from left to right. This activity can lead to writing a story based on the pictures, or writing a description of a sequence of events.

❋ Hot Seat

Seat children in a circle, with one chair being designated the "hot seat." The student in the hot seat portrays a character from a book that has been shared by the class or a historical character. Other students ask him or her questions to find out more about the character's life. You can change the time frames too, moving back into the past or forward into the future. If the character is historical, details must be correct. The hot-seat activity is described more fully in Chapter 5.

❋ Questionnaires

Students can survey their classmates, other students in the school, teachers, or community members to complete questionnaires about a range of topics: favorite types of reading, television programs, eating habits, views about a particular issue, and so on. They can use the information they have gained as a basis for further class work, perhaps involving a quantification or comparison of results, or the questionnaire can be one means of gaining information for a larger project that students are involved with. Apart from giving students practice in asking questions, the activity is also an opportunity for teachers to talk with students about the appropriate ways to do this, taking into account the level of formality that is required in this context as students may be interacting with people they do not know well.

❋ Problem Solving

Contexts for problem solving occur in all curriculum areas. Groups of children must solve a problem by discussion and report back to the class about their solutions. Exercises where students are encouraged to think laterally, in unusual and creative ways that are less bound by the constraints of formal logical thinking, also provide fun contexts for spoken language.

For example, ask the children, in groups, to think about "problems" such as the following:

How can you combine two of the following to make something new: a paintbrush, a wheelbarrow, a garbage bin, four wheels, a spade, a tent?
Possible solution: *Put the tent on the wheels to make a mobile home.*
How many uses can you think of for an old car tire?
Possible solution: *Grow flowers in it; use it as a swing.*

❊ *Paired Problem Solving*

This activity is useful in those situations where something is to be made, such as in art, in design and technology, or in science. In the following example, which is taken from the work of Jenny Des-Fountain and Alan Howe (1992), pairs of students are engaged in two different problem-solving activities, based on a book they have read. One group of pairs is designing a mobile, and the other is designing a boat made out of newspaper that will keep afloat twenty marbles. When the groups have finished, different pairs come together to cross-question each other about what they did, how they did it, and what problems they faced. The group who made the boat had a problem! In the children's words:

> SYLVIA: It kept on sinking, and the newspaper, it kept on . . .
> MANZEER: Leaking.
> SYLVIA: Breaking.

Sylvia and Manzeer continue by describing what they did and what happened. Their first attempt at making the boat had fallen apart. As Manzeer said, "It looked like a bit of food; it was all cut up." The other pair begin to question them about the shape, and one student makes the suggestion that perhaps it should have been flat-bottomed. There is a very real point to this discussion, since the next part of the activity is for each pair to complete the other activity.

This kind of hands-on, problem-solving activity is an excellent one to use with ESL learners. At the stage when the object is being constructed, those with little English can participate on a more equal footing, since this stage of the activity will be less language dependent. As we suggested in Chapter 1, language that is "situation embedded" is easier both to produce and to understand. Second, new language will be heard in context, and it is more likely to be noticed and taken up since the need to use it will be immediate. Third, the activity as a whole can be pitched at an appropriate cognitive level—it is a challenging task that demands critical thinking and problem-solving skills, not simply language "rehearsal."

In addition, during the discussion that follows the hands-on activity, three particular aspects of language are likely to be modeled and reinforced:

1. *Questioning.* The children must ask questions of each other. Here the children asked, "What happened to yours? What happened in the end? Did you make a newspaper boat first? Did you do a flat bottom?" As we noted earlier, in general children have few opportunities to ask questions, and this is a very good opportunity to practice question forms in an authentic context.
2. *Reporting.* The two pairs must report what they did to each other. This requires them to give information to others who did not share in the experience, and thus to use the kind of explicit language discussed earlier. (If the teacher wishes to focus on this, it would also provide an authentic context for using the past tense.)

3. *Making Suggestions.* The discussion requires the listeners to make constructive suggestions. In this case, one of the speakers in the group provided a good model of how to offer a suggestion when she suggested how to improve the design of the boat: "Do you think you should have done a flat bottom?" As discussed earlier, this kind of language is not necessarily just "picked up" by ESL students, and the context of this activity would be an excellent one for the teacher to focus on some specific ways of making suggestions: "Do you think you should . . . Maybe you could . . . How about if you had . . . Perhaps it would be better if . . ." This could be a focus in the initial setting up of the activity as a whole.

Note that this activity exemplifies a number of principles for well-designed group work in an ESL classroom: there is a real need to talk, and an authentic purpose for it; it has a built-in information gap, since pairs hold different information; all children are involved; it is cognitively demanding; and it is embedded in a curriculum topic that the children have been studying.

Activities Especially for Beginners

Again, all of these activities can be integrated with particular subject topics.

✳ *Inquiry and Elimination*

(Practices question forms and helps develop logical thinking.)
Choose a large picture showing a range of objects within a set, such as a picture showing a number of different animals. One member of the group chooses an animal and the others must guess which one it is by asking yes/no questions only. It's important to restrict the number of questions that can be asked so that guesses are not just random. Instead, encourage children to ask those questions that elicit the maximum amount of information. For example, the answer *yes* to the question *does it fly* immediately eliminates all those animals that don't fly.

✳ *I'm Thinking Of . . .*

(Practices describing things and their functions, use of that.)
Use a set of pictures of objects related to a particular topic being studied, such as sets of dinosaur pictures, animals, tools, food, forms of transport. Each student in the group says "I'm thinking of something that is . . ." and then proceeds to describe the object. Whoever guesses the object then takes the next turn.

✳ *Describe and Draw*

(Practices giving instructions, describing objects, describing position—under, near, next to, to the left of, etc.)

Children work in pairs, and each has a blank sheet of paper and drawing materials. Child A describes to Child B what she or he is drawing, and Child B reproduces the drawing according to A's description. This is a barrier game—they should not be able to see each other's work.

※ **Find My Partner**

(Practices question forms and describing.)

Deal out to the group four to six pictures, two of which are identical, with the others having minor differences. Pictures can be related to a curriculum topic. One of the two identical pictures should be marked with an X, and whoever is dealt that card has to find the other picture by questioning other members of the group. (See Figure 2–4.)

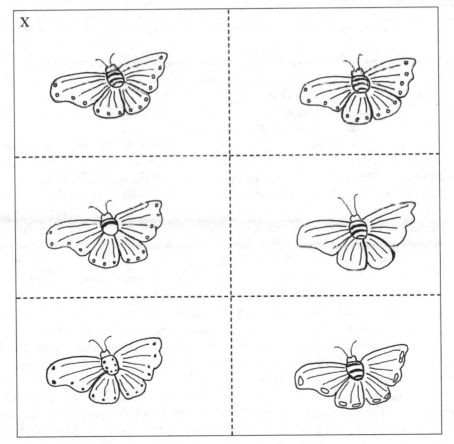

FIGURE 2–4. *Find My Partner*

❋ *What Did You See?*

(Practices vocabulary.)

On a table, place a selection of objects, or pictures of objects, that are related to a topic being studied. After children have looked at them for a few moments, cover the objects with a cloth, and see how many objects children can remember.

Finally, as a general checklist for pair and group activities, consider these points:

- Is talking really necessary for the task or activity to be completed?
- Are content areas of the curriculum being reinforced?
- Are children using stretches of language?
- Is thinking involved?
- Are all children involved in some way?

Talking with Children

So far, we have focused on the advantages of using group work in the classroom. But there will be times when the whole class works together, with the teacher in traditional position at the front of the class. Often, as we have suggested, the kind of interaction in which teacher and students commonly engage in such situations is not supportive of ESL development, in that children get fewer chances to speak, and say little when they do. However, even in teacher-centered situations, interactions can be modified to allow for a more equal distribution of speaking rights.

In Chapter 1, we saw how the notion of a zone of proximal development presents learning as something accomplished through collaboration. The more experienced participant supports the less experienced participant with those aspects of the task that the learner is not yet able to do alone. In the example shown in Figure 2–5, children are taking part in what I call **teacher-guided reporting**. It refers to those times when a student is asked to report to the whole class about what he or she has done or learned. It's probably an activity that you use yourself; you may refer to it as "reporting back" or "reporting to the class" or "reviewing."

Here the term teacher-*guided* reporting is adopted to make more explicit the role of the teacher in providing scaffolding for the learner. Children may not always find it easy to explain clearly to others what they have done or learned, and for ESL learners in particular, this may be a daunting task that pushes them beyond what they are able to do alone in English. In teacher-guided reporting, the teacher provides scaffolding by clarifying, questioning, and providing models for the speaker, so that the learner and teacher together collaboratively build up what the learner wants to say. Just as the father and mother provided interactional scaffolding to Nigel in the "goat text," whereby he was able to reach further in his language than he could have done alone, so too can a teacher provide scaffolding for learners so that the interaction becomes a supportive context for second language development.

	Student	Teacher	Commentary
1		what did you find out?	*T. opens with an open question*
2	if you put a nail . onto the piece of foil . . and then pick it . pick it up . . the magnet will . . . . that if you put a . nail . under a piece of foil . and then pick . pick the foil up with the magnet . . still . still with the nail . . under it . . . it won't		
3		it what?	*It what? = it does what? T. is looking for a verb*
4	it won't/ it won't come out		
5		what won't come out?	*What = what does it refer to?*
6	it'll go up		
7		wait just a minute . . can you explain that a bit more, Loretta?	*T. asks L. to clarify*
8	like if you put a nail and then foil over it and then put the nail on top . of the foil . . the nail underneath the foil . Miss, I can't say it		
9		no, you're doing fine I . I can see	*T. encourages L. Affirms she understands what L is trying to say.*
10	Miss, forget about the magnet/ em the magnet holds it with the foil up the top and the nail's underneath and the foil's on top and put the magnet in it and		

FIGURE 2–5. *Teacher-Guided Reporting (1)*   (continued)

	Student	Teacher	Commentary
	you lift it up . . and the nail will em . . . hold it/stick with the magnet and the foil's in between		
11		oh . so even with the foil in between . the . magnet will still pick up the nail . alright does the magnet pick up the foil?	T. "recasts" what L has said.
12	no		

FIGURE 2–5. *Teacher-Guided Reporting (1) (continued)*

In the classroom dialogue shown in Figure 2–5, the more experienced participant (the teacher) supports the less experienced participant (the student) to carry out a demanding language task (reporting to the class). Loretta, the student, had been separating a number of objects into magnetic and nonmagnetic groups. She had discovered first that a nail was magnetic and that aluminum foil was not. She had then placed a piece of aluminum foil between a magnet and a nail, discovering that the magnet still attracted the nail.

Explaining this makes considerable linguistic demands on Loretta, and she clearly finds it very difficult to verbalize what she wants to say. Her comment in Turn 8, "Miss, I can't say it," gives some indication of just how difficult the task is for her. Also note how much she pauses and how "hesitant" she appears. As you read, consider how the teacher provides scaffolding for the learner, so that with this guidance, Loretta is able to complete the task successfully. Notice too the overall pattern; although this is in one sense a "teacher-controlled" interaction, the teacher doesn't dominate—as you can see from the text, the learner says far more than the teacher.

In terms of language development, this exchange with the teacher is very supportive for Loretta. Each of her three attempts to report what she has done (2, 8, 10) become progressively less hesitant and more understandable, with the last attempt being a greatly improved version of her initial attempt (2). How does the teacher support the learner to make this happen?

First, the teacher begins with an open question to which there is no pre-scripted reply. Although the teacher knows in general what Loretta has done, it is left to Loretta herself to initiate what she wants to talk about. In other words, she enters the conversation on her own terms. In general, it is a much easier task for learners to initiate what they want to talk about than to respond to what someone else wants them to talk about. Second, the teacher provides very specific scaffolding on precisely those language items that need to be clarified for the listeners: the action being referred to (3) and the thing being referred to (5). She gives a word of encouragement, but she resists recasting or rewording what Loretta has said until the eleventh turn in the conversation. This added time allows Loretta two more attempts to explain what she is trying to say and more opportunity to focus on *how* she is expressing it.

What can be learned from this exchange? First, it is important to find a balance between straight "display" questions and those that allow learners to negotiate what they want to say. When you are questioning children about what they have learned, possible openers could include:

> *Tell us what you learned.*
> *Tell us about what you did.*
> *What did you find out?*
> *What would you like to tell us about?*
> *What did you find most interesting?*

Try monitoring your own talk to see what openers you use most often.

Second, it is important to SLOW DOWN the dialogue. This *doesn't* mean that you should speak more slowly, but that the overall pace of the discourse should allow sufficient time for learners to think about what they are saying, and thus how they are saying it. This can be achieved in two ways. First, you can increase "wait time"—that is, the time you wait for the learner to respond. Increasing this by just an extra couple of seconds makes a big difference to how much students say, how clearly they say it, and how much they are able to demonstrate what they understand. Second, you can allow more turns before you evaluate or recast (reword) what the learner has said. The teacher in the transcript shown in Figure 2–5 made a significant choice: she could have recast what the student was attempting to say at Turn 3 but chose not to, instead waiting until Turn 11. She thus allowed the student to have several attempts, offering much more opportunity for student output. She uses a simple strategy, which is to ask the student to clarify meaning rather than take responsibility for doing this herself. Her responses to the student do not simply evaluate what the student has said; instead, they prompt the student to have another go: "Can you explain that a bit more?" Teachers can also do this by saying things like:

> *Can you say that again?*
> *I don't quite understand. Can you tell me that again?*
> *Tell me a little more.*
> *Can you just expand on that a little more?*
> *What do you mean?*
> *Can you explain it again?*

Whenever you say something like this, you are slowing down the pace of the discourse, because you are giving learners a chance to formulate, as far as they are able, a more explicit way of saying what they want to say. And there is considerable evidence that learners who have more opportunities to reflect on and improve their own communication receive more long-term benefits for language learning than those who constantly have communication problems solved for them by the teacher. Of course, you need to use your own judgment in relation to individual learners, and decide how much responsibility for clarification you put onto them, but almost certainly most ESL students will be able to say more if they are given more time during the process of an interaction.

Third, it is important to respond to meaning. This involves really listening to what the students say, rather than waiting for the answer you would like them to give! While the teacher's scaffolding in this example could be seen as a focus on form—that is, on the grammar and structure of the language—everything that she says is ultimately in the service of meaning making, not for the sake of practicing grammar. As Lily Wong-Fillmore (1985) says in her study of effective teachers of very young ESL students, the teachers "were effective communicators . . . because all of them were concerned with communication" (40).

In Summary—Making It Happen

In this chapter we have seen that both student-student and teacher-student talk can provide rich contexts for second language development. But just allowing talk to occur is not enough. Productive talk does not just happen—it needs to be deliberately and systematically planned, just as we plan for literacy events. Julianna's comment in Chapter 1—"I can say what I want, but not for school work and strangers"—reminds us that developing a language for learning is not a matter of chance. How tasks are designed, how group work is set up, and how teachers respond to students all impact on how effective classroom talk is in supporting language development. And sometimes, as we have seen, even quite small changes in how opportunities for talk are set up can have significant effects on how the discourse is played out. It is not an exaggeration to suggest that classroom talk determines whether or not children learn, and their ultimate feelings of self-worth as students. Talk is how education happens!

Suggestions for Further Reading

Cook, S. 1998. *Collaborative Learning Activities in the Classroom: Designing Inclusive Materials for Learning and Language Development.* Leicester, UK: Resource Centre for Multicultural Education.

Corson, D. 1993. "Language Policy and Minority Culture." Chapter 3 in *Language, Minority Education and Gender,* ed. D. Corson. Clevedon, UK: Multilingual Matters.

McGroarty, M. 1992. "Cooperative Learning: The Benefits for Content-Area Teaching." In *The Multicultural Classroom*, ed. P. Richard-Amato and M. Snow. New York: Longman.

McGroarty, M. 1993. "Cooperative Learning and Language Acquisition." In *Cooperative Learning: A Response to Linguistic and Cultural Diversity*, ed. D. Holt. Washington, DC: Center for Applied Linguistics.

3

From Speaking to Writing in the Content Classroom

Prior experience becomes a context for interpreting the new experience . . . prior experiences serve as the contexts within which the language being used is to be understood. Lily Wong-Fillmore, "When Does Teacher Talk Work as Input?"

Using the Mode Continuum

In Chapter 1, I briefly touched on the idea of register. One of the ways we looked at this was to compare four short science texts. Here are four similar texts again, this time as more extended pieces of language. They illustrate how certain linguistic features change as language becomes increasingly closer to written forms.

Text 1: (spoken by three 10-year-old students, with accompanying action)
this . . . no, it doesn't go . . . it doesn't move . . . try that . . . yes, it does . . . a bit . . . that won't . . . won't work, it's not metal . . . these are the best . . . going really fast.

Text 2: (spoken by one student about the action, after the event)
we tried a pin . . . a pencil sharpener . . . some iron filings and a piece of plastic . . . the magnet didn't attract the pin.

Text 3: (written by the same student)
Our experiment was to find out what a magnet attracted. We discovered that a magnet attracts some kinds of metal. It attracted the iron filings, but not the pin.

Text 4: (taken from a child's encyclopedia)
A magnet . . . is able to pick up, or attract, a piece of steel or iron because its magnetic field flows into the magnet, turning it into a temporary magnet. Magnetic attraction occurs only between ferrous materials.

As discussed in Chapter 1, the term *mode* is used in Halliday's functional linguistics to refer to the channel of communication, whether it is spoken or written. The four texts shown here together form a continuum from spoken to written language. Using Martin's (1984) term, we will refer to this sequence as a *mode continuum.*

Text 1 is typical of the kind of situation-embedded language produced in face-to-face contexts. The fact that everyone can see what is being talked about means that objects need not be named—instead, a speaker can use reference words (such as *this, these, that*), to verbally "point" to things in the immediate environment and know that the other participants in the conversation will understand what is being referred to.

In Text 2 the context changes because the student is telling others what she learned and no longer has the science equipment in front of her. She must now reconstruct the experience through language alone, so she makes explicit the things or people she is referring to (*we, pin, pencil sharpener, iron filings, piece of plastic*) and names what is happening (*attract.*)

Reconstructing Experience Through Language Alone

Text 3 is a written text and, since the audience is now unseen, the writer can't rely on shared assumptions: she can't assume that readers of the text will know anything at all about the particular events she is describing. So, once again, the writer must recreate the experience through language alone, but this time she also needs to provide an orientation for the readers in order to provide a context for what follows: *Our experiment was to . . .*

In Text 4 there is no reference to a specific experiment. The magnet referred to here as *a magnet* is generic: its properties are those of all magnets. There is an increase in technical terms and in the density of the text; a lot of information is being packed in. One way of packing in information in a written text is to use a *nominalization*, meaning that a process or verb (*attract*) is turned into a noun (*attraction*). Turning processes into nouns is typical of much written language because it is very often the general concept or phenomenon we want to talk about, rather than the people and processes around a specific event.

While spoken and written language obviously have distinctive characteristics, this continuum of texts illustrates that there is no absolute boundary between them. Technology increases this blurring. Leaving a detailed message on an answering machine, for example, may be quite linguistically demanding since, in the absence of two-way contact, and without (initially at least) the shared understandings and expectations that are implicit in two-way, face-to-face communication, we are required to "speak aloud" the kind of language that would more usually be written. Thus in terms of the mode continuum, it is perhaps more appropriate to describe texts as "more spoken-like" or "more written-like," and these are the terms that will be used here.

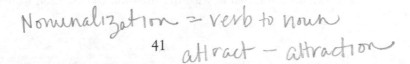

Nominalization = verb to noun
attract — attraction

As discussed briefly in Chapter 1, texts that are most spoken-like (like Text 1) are often dependent for their interpretation on the situation in which they occur: they are situation-embedded. More written-like texts are not embedded in the situation itself; they must be complete enough in themselves to create their own context for the listener or reader. Thus as we move along the mode continuum, texts are no longer dependent on the situation in which they occur: if we read a book while at the beach, for example, our understanding of what we read and how we interpret the language usually has nothing to do with the fact that we are sitting on a beach.

As Chapter 1 pointed out, a second language learner is likely to have fewer difficulties with producing something like Text 1, where the situational context itself provides a support for meaning and there are thus fewer linguistic demands, than with more written-like texts, where more lexico-grammatical resources are required (those involving grammar and vocabulary). It is worth noting, too, that when children are expected to write simply on the basis of personal experiences, they are being asked to take a very large linguistic step (as can be seen by comparing Texts 1 and 3), and one that is beyond the current linguistic resources of some second language learners. If you reflect back on the spoken language activities described in the previous chapter, you'll see that many of them require learners to use more explicit spoken language (like Text 2). This is the reason, for example, why barrier games such as *Find the Difference* are designed the way they are. If students were to show each other their pictures, they would be using language as in Text 1; by not showing each other the pictures, they are using language more like Text 2, and thus are practicing a more written-like register.

In this chapter we will look at how one teacher used the notion of the mode continuum as a major organizing principle in the planning of her classroom program. (For a fuller description of this program, see Gibbons 2001.) For all but two of her students, English was a second or subsequent language, and therefore her whole curriculum needed to be supportive of language development as well as to focus on appropriate content. Using the mode continuum as a linguistic framework, she designed teaching activities that were sequenced from most situation-embedded, or most spoken-like (and thus for ESL learners the most easily understood), to least situation-dependent, or most written-like (a written journal). A major focus for the teacher was to help students use spoken language in the way that Text 2 illustrates—that is, spoken language that is not dependent on the immediate situational context in which it occurs. This more written-like spoken language serves as a language bridge between the talk associated with experiential activities and the more formal—and often written—registers of the curriculum.

Based on the science topic of magnetism, the teacher planned teaching and learning activities to reflect points along the mode continuum so as to offer a logical development in terms of language learning. Here are the stages that the children moved through:

1. *Doing an experiment (small groups).* Learners initially participated in small-group learning experiences based on a number of science experiments in which the language used was tied in with the situation the children were in. What they

talked about referred directly to the actions in which they were taking part, and to what was happening in front of them.

2. *Introducing key vocabulary (whole class)*. At this point the teacher briefly introduced the words *attract* and *repel* to the children.

3. *Teacher-guided reporting (whole class)*. Groups of students, with the help of the teacher, shared their learning with the whole class. Since this did not involve the use of the concrete materials, students had to use language more explicitly, which provided a linguistic bridge into journal writing. During this part of the cycle, the teacher also helped the children build up generalizations by directing children's attention to the commonalties in each group's findings.

4. *Journal writing (individual)*. This was the final activity of the cycle and linguistically the most demanding.

This cycle was repeated several times during the unit on magnets.

The stages are described in more detail in the following section, together with examples of the language the children used. You will see that the children gradually learn to use language in ways that are more appropriate to the context they are in (learning and talking about science). Note as well the role that the teacher-learner talk plays in this development.

Stage 1: Doing an Experiment

In many elementary schools, it is usual for students to rotate through a number of activities over the course of one or two lessons. However, as suggested in Chapter 2, this kind of organizational structure negates any authentic purpose for reporting back to others, since children are likely to have shared very similar experiences. Here, the teacher made an attempt to set up a genuine communicative situation by having each group of children work at different (though related) science experiments. And so, by the time they had completed their experiments, each group of children held different information from other class members. In its communicative structure, the classroom organization was based on what we referred to in the previous chapter as an information "gap," so that there was an authentic exchange of information at the reporting stage.

The children were carrying out the experiment described in Chapter 2. Prior to beginning the activity, they were told that they would later describe, and attempt to explain, to the rest of the class what happened. The texts that follow occurred as students were engaged in this activity.

Text 1

HANNAH:	try . . . the other way
MARCO:	like that
HANNAH:	north pole facing down
JOANNA:	we tried that
DANIELLA:	oh!

HANNAH: it stays up!

MARCO: magic!

DANIELLA: let's show the others

JOANNA: mad!

DANIELLA: I'll put north pole facing north pole . . . see what happen

MARCO: that's what we just did

DANIELLA: yeah . . . like this . . . look

[The dialogue continues for several minutes longer as the students try different positions for the magnet, and then they begin to formulate an explanation.]

HANNAH: can I try that? . . . I know why . . . I know why . . . that's like . . because the north pole is on this side and that north pole's there . . . so they don't stick together

DANIELLA: what . . like this? yeah

HANNAH: yeah . . see because the north pole on this side . but turn it on the other . . this side like that . . . turn it that way . . yeah

DANIELLA: and it will stick

HANNAH: and it will stick because . look . . the north pole's on that side because . .

DANIELLA: the north pole's on that side yeah

At this stage, the children do not know the terms *attract* and *repel*. Instead, they use familiar words like *stick* or *push away*. (Sometimes this led to very interesting comments—one child was overheard to say, as he was holding two magnets that were repelling each other, "It feels like a strong wind!")

What can we learn from this example? First, we can see again how small-group work supports learning. Together children explored and developed certain scientific understandings, namely that the position of the poles is significant in how the magnets behave. They also attempted to hypothesize about the causal relations involved (note the use of the connectives *so, because*). So, even though they were not using what we might think of as science language, they were learning a lot about science. As the discourse progresses, individual utterances became longer and more explicit, and this occurred as the students began to formulate explanations for what they saw. The teacher's instruction to "try to explain what you see" was significant here, since it extended the task from simply "doing" to "doing and thinking." Wegerif and Mercer (1996) suggest that it is through this kind of exploratory talk "that knowledge begins to be built up and reasoning is made more visible" (51). This piece of learning later became shared knowledge when the children reported to the rest of the class, and was the basis upon which the teacher next introduced subject-specific vocabulary such as *attract* and *repel*.

Stage 2: Introducing Key Vocabulary

Before the children reported to the rest of the class, the teacher introduced a new vocabulary item, drawing on the experiences the children have just had and at the same time demonstrating the meanings physically:

> now I'm going to give you another word for what Joseph was trying to say one more scientific word . some of you were saying it pushes away . . . or slips off . . . so instead of saying the magnet pushes away I'm going to give you a new word . . . *repel* [said with emphasis] . it actually means to push away from you [demonstrating with her arm] . *repel.*

From the point of view of second language learning, it is important to note that in this classroom the children were given an opportunity to develop some understandings about magnets *before* they were expected to understand and use more scientific discourse. It is not until after the group work that the teacher introduced the scientific terms *attract* and *repel*—that is, at a time when students had already expressed these meanings in familiar everyday language. There is some parallel here to the principle within bilingual programs that suggests that learning should occur first in the mother tongue as a basis to learning in the second language, but here the issue is one of register rather than language.

Stage 3: Teacher-Guided Reporting

Science educator Rosalind Driver (1983) makes the important point that "activity by itself is not enough. It is the sense that is made of it that matters" (49). In teacher-guided reporting, the teacher talks with the children to help them make sense of the activities in which they have been engaged. Wegerif and Mercer (1996) suggest that as children are encouraged and enabled "to clearly describe events, to account for outcomes and consolidate what they have learned *in words*," they are helped to "understand and gain access to educated discourse" (53, emphasis added).

In the classroom example shown here, the overall aim of the teacher-guided reporting was to extend children's linguistic resources and focus on aspects of the specific discourse of science. As the teacher expressed it to the children, "Now we're trying to talk like scientists." She also anticipated that the reporting stage would create a context for students to "rehearse" language structures that were closer to written discourse—that is, that were closer to the written end of the mode continuum.

In the text shown in Figure 3–1, Hannah is explaining what she learned. The teacher's role in guided reporting is of course crucial; the text provides an example of how her interactions with individual students provided a scaffold for their attempts, allowing for communication to proceed while giving the learners access to new ways of expressing the meanings they wanted to make.

	Student	Teacher
1		try to tell them what you learned . . . OK . . . (*to Hannah*) yes?
2	when I put/ when you put . . . when you put a magnet . . . on top of a magnet and the north pole poles are . . . . (*7-second pause, Hannah is clearly having difficulty expressing what she wants to say*)	
3		yes yes you're doing fine . . you put one magnet on top of another . .
4	and and the north poles are together er em the magnet . . . repels the magnet er . . . the magnet and the other magnet . . . sort of floats in the air?	
5		I think that was very well told. . . very well told . . do you have anything to add to that Charlene? (*The teacher invites other contributions, and then asks Hannah to explain it again.*)
6		now listen . . now Hannah explain once more . . . alright Hannah . . . excuse me everybody (*regaining class's attention*) . . listen again to her explanation
7	the two north poles are leaning together and the magnet on the bottom is repelling the magnet on top so that the magnet on the top is sort of . . . floating in the air	
8		so that these two magnets are repelling (*said with emphasis*) each other and . . . (*demonstrating*) look at the force of it.

FIGURE 3–1. *Teacher-Guided Reporting (2)*

This interaction between teacher and student is different in several small but important respects from the traditional IRF pattern, which was discussed in Chapter 2. Typically, the IRF pattern occurs in fairly predictable ways, frequently involving a question to which the teacher already knows the answer, followed by a student answer (often brief), and finally a teacher evaluation relating to the correctness (or otherwise) of the answer. For the most part, teachers' questions are often framed in ways that do not allow for students to make extended responses (Dillon 1990). In contrast, in the text shown in Figure 3–1, the interactions approximate more closely what occurs in mother-tongue, adult-child interactions outside of the formal teaching context (see, for example, Halliday 1975; Painter 1985).

During teacher-guided reporting, the teacher begins the exchange by inviting students to relate what they have learned, rather than with a known answer or display question. In this way, the teacher sets up a context that allows the students to initiate the specific topic of the exchange. As Ellis (1994) shows, when learners initiate what they wish to talk about, language learning is facilitated because they enter the discourse on their own terms, rather than responding to a specific request for information from the teacher. In the text shown in Figure 3–1, the student takes on the role of "expert." Although the teacher is in control of the knowledge associated with the overall thematic development of the topic, the individual exchanges locate that control in the student.

This increase in the equality of teacher and student roles leads Hannah to produce longer stretches of discourse than often occurs in classroom interaction. The teacher can be described as "leading from behind." At the same time, while the teacher follows Hannah's lead and accepts as a valid contribution the information the child gives, she also recasts or reformulates what Hannah says, modeling alternative forms of language that are more appropriate in the context of talking about science.

From the perspective of second language learning, it as clear that teacher-guided reporting encourages learner language to be "pushed." Hannah is going beyond what is unproblematic for her, but, because she is allowed a second attempt, she has an additional opportunity for comprehensible output (see Chapter 2). Hannah's second attempt at her explanation is considerably less hesitant and syntactically more complete than her first, and it is produced this time without the help of the teacher. As I discussed in Chapter 1, Vygotsky (1978) suggests that learning occurs, with support from those more expert, at the learner's zone of proximal development—that is, at the "outer edges" of a learner's current abilities. In Turn 2, Hannah appears to have reached her own zone of proximal development for this task, since she hesitates for a considerable time and can presumably go no further alone. The recasting and support she receives from the teacher (Turn 3) is precisely timed for learning to occur and to assist Hannah to continue with what she wants to say.

As this text illustrates, the reporting context also gives students opportunities to produce longer stretches of discourse that are more written-like than those that occurred in the small-group work. Often this required the teacher to increase wait time, on occasions for as long as eight seconds. Research suggests that when teachers ask questions of students, they typically wait one second or less for the students to begin a reply, but that when teachers wait for three or more seconds, there are significant changes in student use of language and in the attitudes and expectations of both students and teachers (Rowe 1986). It would seem likely that increased wait time is even more important for students who are formulating responses in a language they do not fully control. Perhaps equally important, we can see from these interactions that students are able to complete what they want to say successfully: they are positioned as successful interactants and learners. In addition, since it is the immediate need of the learner that is influencing to a large extent the teacher's choice of actual wording, it seems likely that this wording will be more salient to the learner—more likely to be taken note of—than if it had occurred in a context that was less immediate.

Another significant mode shift occurred toward the end of most reporting sessions, where the teacher used children's personal knowledge to show how generalizations might be generated. For example, her questions at this point included:

Can you see something in common with all these experiences?
What's the same about all these experiments?

Such questions require the students to do more than simply produce a personal recount of what they did; they must now express their learning in terms of generalizations. Note how in the examples below, the children no longer mention themselves in the discourse:

the north pole of the magnet sticks . . attracts . the second magnet . the south pole of the second magnet.

if you put the south and north together then they will . . attract but if you put north and north or south and south . together . . they won't stick . attract.

The teacher-guided reporting stage, then, both in the way language is used and in the ways that children are encouraged to generalize from their learning, serves to create a bridge for learners between personal ways of understanding a phenomenon and everyday language, and the broader concepts and language associated with the science curriculum.

Stage 4: Journal Writing

After the students had taken part in the reporting session, they wrote a response in their journals to the question, "What have you learned?" These responses later served as a source of information in the writing of more formal reports about magnets. What is particularly significant is that these journals indicated that the talk with the teacher had influenced the way the students wrote: the students' writing reflected wordings that they had used in interaction with the teacher, or that had been part of the teacher's recasting. This was particularly evident when the students themselves had had opportunity to reformulate their *own* talk. Here, for example, is what Hannah wrote:

I found it very interesting that when you stuck at least 8 paddle pop sticks in a piece of polystyrene, and then put a magnet with the North and South pole in the oval and put another magnet with the north and south pole on top, the magnet on the bottom will repel the magnet on the top and the magnet on the top would look like it is floating in the air.

And here is an excerpt from the journal writing of a student who had *listened* to the talk between Hannah and the teacher. The conversation influenced her writing too.

The thing made out of polystyrene with paddle pop sticks, one group put one magnet facing north and another magnet on top facing north as well and they repelled each other. It looked like the top magnet was floating up in the air.

In Summary

While this teacher's program illustrates the value of learning by doing (especially for second language learners where concrete experiences help make language comprehensible), it also illustrates the critical role of teacher-student talk in children's learning and language development. Regular teacher-guided reporting is one way of providing an authentic and meaningful context for students to develop the more academic registers of school.

We can also see that it is not simply the linguistic features of language itself that affect students' comprehension (for example the simplicity or otherwise of the grammatical structures), but also the previous knowledge they bring to the new language they are hearing. Note that in this classroom the new language introduced by the teacher occurred *after* students had already developed some understanding of key concepts through the small-group work, and so new language was more readily interpretable by the students. What preceded this new language—in this case the learning that the students had gained through their participation in the small-group work—was therefore an important factor in students' understanding of it and their ultimate ability to use it.

One implication of this for teaching is that language that would normally be beyond students' comprehension is much more likely to be understood when students can bring their experiences and understandings as a basis for interpretation. This broad principle is illustrated at other points in this book, in particular in the chapters on reading and listening. In the words of Wong-Fillmore (1985) at the beginning of this chapter, written in relation to her study of kindergarten ESL learners, "prior experiences serve as the contexts within which the language being used is to be understood" (31).

This overall sequence of activities also presents a challenge to more traditional ways of sequencing teaching and learning activities in the second language classroom, where a new topic very often *begins* with the pre-teaching of vocabulary or a grammatical structure. While this approach may certainly be appropriate at times, it is worth remembering that it is underpinned by the notion that learners must first "learn" language before they can "use" it. As we have seen, however, ESL learners must from the outset use their second language for curriculum learning, and they need many contexts in which they can do this. In this class, students used their current language resources at the beginning of the unit while the focus on new language occurred at later stages, a sequence that allowed for students to build on their existing understandings and language, and to link old learning with new. In effect, they moved successfully *toward* the language of the curriculum, throughout the unit of work, rather than being expected to master it prior to their learning of science.

Suggestions for Further Reading

CUMMINS, J. 2000. "Language Proficiency in Academic Contexts." Chapter 3 in *Language, Power and Pedagogy: Bilingual Children in the Crossfire*, ed. J. Cummins. Clevedon, UK: Multilingual Matters.

EDWARDS, D., and MERCER, N. 1987. "Ritual and Principle." Chapter 6 in *Common Knowledge: The Development of Understanding in the Classroom*, ed. D. Edwards and N. Mercer. London: Methuen.

GIBBONS, P. 2001. "Learning a New Register in a Second Language." In *English Language Teaching in Its Social Context*, ed. Candlin C. and N. Mercer. London: Routledge.

HALLIDAY, M. 1993. "Towards a Language-Based Theory of Learning." *Linguistics and Education* 5: 93–116.

MARTIN, J. 1984. "Language, Register and Genre." In *Children Writing: Study Guide*, ed. F. Christie. Geelong, Victoria, AU: Deakin University Press.

4

Writing in a Second Language Across the Curriculum
An Integrated Approach

To be alert to the ways one's language works for creat-
ing and organizing meaning is to be conscious of how
to manipulate and use it.   Frances Christie, "The
Changing Face of Literacy"

Changing Expectations

Literacy in today's world is a very different thing from literacy as it was understood in
the nineteenth century and in the early part of the twentieth century. At the beginning of the nineteenth century, literacy was valued largely because it taught the capacity to read the Bible and other improving works, and many children, once they had left
school, were required to do little more than write their name. As late as the 1930s, the
level of literacy required was still quite minimal, and was represented by the capacity
to read and copy simple passages and to write an occasional short text, such as a letter or a passage on a given topic (Christie 1990).

By contrast, the contemporary world in the early part of the twenty-first century
demands a level of sophistication in literacy skills greater than ever before, and "those
who do not possess considerable literacy will be effectively 'locked out' from so much
of the knowledge, information and ideas that are part of the culture of the society"
(Christie 1990, 20). In addition, those leaving school without an appropriate level of
literacy will be competing for a rapidly diminishing pool of unskilled jobs; as Christie
points out, the relationship between illiteracy, social alienation, and poverty is too
acute to be ignored. Today's children are entering a world in which they will need to
be able to read and think critically, to live and work in intercultural contexts, to solve
new kinds of problems, and to be flexible in ever-changing work contexts; in short, to
make informed decisions about their own lives and their role in a multicultural society. We cannot opt out of the Western print world and remain active participants in
society.

Among those who are potentially disadvantaged because of difficulties in learning to control written English are those who are learning it as a second language. This is particularly likely when learners have not previously developed literacy skills in their mother tongue (Cummins 1996). This chapter discusses some of the difficulties that ESL students may have in learning to write in English, and it suggests a teaching cycle that models and makes explicit some of the major forms of writing, or text types, used in school.

Learning to Write in a Second Language

First, drawing on your knowledge of your own students, consider in general terms some of the characteristics of good writers and less effective writers. Effective writers are likely to think about and plan their writing, at least in a general way, before they begin. They understand that writing is a recursive process—that writers continually revise and edit at all stages of the writing process, from first draft to final product. They are also able to anticipate reader problems. For example, they make clear what reference words such as *he* and *she* refer to. They are aware of the linguistic differences between writing and speaking (such as those discussed in Chapter 2), and know that written language is not just speech written down. And they understand how to organize the ideas and writing of the text as a whole. By contrast, less effective writers probably do none of these things. They may focus primarily on the mechanics of writing, such as the spelling, and are overly concerned with "correctness." As a result, they may lack confidence to write at length or in new ways. They tend not to plan at a whole-text level, and they are less able to anticipate the language and content information that a reader will require in order to fully understand their writing. Their writing tends to sound like "speech written down," and they probably have difficulty in revising and editing their own work.

Young students learning to write in their second language have even more to learn about writing. Literacy teaching in Western schools usually presupposes that children have already developed spoken language skills in the relevant language, and have internalized considerable understandings about how to use the language. But this may not be the case for ESL students. Trying to grasp concepts of print—such as sound-symbol relationships, directionality, and the notion that written symbols are not arbitrary but fixed—is obviously much more difficult in a language in which you are not strong. ESL students are also less likely to be familiar with the particular organizational structure of different kinds of writing, and with the grammatical structures of English. Some may be faced with learning a new script or alphabet system. In the next section we'll look at some of the types of writing that are common in school, and consider some of the cultural and linguistic knowledge that is needed in order to produce these forms successfully.

A Genre Approach to Teaching Writing

Different forms of literary writing are often referred to as *genres*, such as poems, plays, or novels, and these general distinctions are often further categorized: adventure novels, detective novels, romance novels, and so on. However, the word has also been used with a much broader meaning, to refer to the range of ways in which things get done in a particular society or culture (Martin 1989; Christie 1990). Under this broader definition, the notion of genre would encompass things as diverse as the TV news, a marriage service, a game show, a lesson, a joke, a telephone conversation with a friend, a newspaper report, or a set of written instructions. Every genre has a number of characteristics that make it different from other genres: a genre has a specific purpose; a particular overall structure; specific linguistic features; and is shared by members of the culture. Most important, members of the culture recognize it as a genre (even though they probably don't use the term!). Let's look briefly at each of these characteristics in turn.

A Specific Purpose

Each of the examples just listed has a specific social purpose or goal—to give information about the current news, for people to be married, to provide amusement, to teach students, and so on. This social purpose is reflected in the way that the genre is structured. A set of instructions, such as a recipe, which is intended to tell someone how to do something, will be organized in sequence, so that each step follows from the one before. Genres, then, are goal-oriented.

A Particular Overall Structure

Every genre has a particular structure. For example, a news program usually begins with the most important and recent news, which may often include reports on international events; goes on to less important, domestic, or local news; and concludes with a sport's review and the weather forecast. If a news program started with a minor piece of news, or with the weather forecast, it would be unexpected. Similarly, if a joke started with the punch line, we would probably no longer consider it a joke.

Specific Linguistic Features

Every genre has particular linguistic features in common with, or very similar to, other genres of the same type. For example, most newspaper reports are likely to make use of the past tense, to name particular people and events, and to say when the particular event took place. They are also likely to include a quotation or two from key participants in the event. Sets of instructions will contain action verbs, and often make use of the imperative. My set of computer instructions, for example, contains the verbs *click, drag, open, type, use, insert, shut down,* and *connect,* and it includes sentences like "Type what you want to find and click 'Search.'"

Shared by Members of the Culture

Genres are cultural, and though similar social purposes (such as writing a business letter) are carried out in many cultures, the way of doing it may look very different from culture to culture. As Chapter 1 pointed out, knowing the context of culture is a part of being able to understand and use language appropriately. Some years ago I received a letter from overseas that began:

> I am immensely delighted and profoundly honoured to send you this letter. Please accept my deepest esteem, my warmest, kindest regards, and sincerest wishes of constant happiness, good health, and ever-increasing prosperity and success in all your endeavours . . .

Four paragraphs later it concluded:

> Deeply grateful to you for each second you have so graciously spent reading my letter. Please do accept once more my profoundest esteem, deepest thanks for your gracious attention and consideration, and my most genuinely sincere wishes of constant happiness, success, peace, and prosperity, now and in the future.

The writer was requesting a copy of a book. The letter was completely accurate in terms of the grammar, but in terms of how it would be judged by a writer from an English-speaking country, the language sounds excessively flowery, ornate, and even servile. In the writer's culture, however, such language is entirely appropriate, whereas the kinds of request letters that someone growing up in an Anglo-Saxon culture might write would be seen as very impolite and abrupt. Similarly, though all cultures have ways of greeting, these ways need to be learned. We may greet each other with a simple, "Hi, how are you?" In some cultures, however, you would be thought very impolite if you did not first ask after each of the other person's family members. So, more than just correct grammar is involved here. What learners must also know is the most *appropriate* language to use and the most *appropriate* ways to get things done. For language teaching purposes, "a useful way of viewing a culture is in terms . . . of its purposeful activities" (Painter 1988). Learning a second language thus means learning the different kinds of spoken and written genres needed to participate in the second language culture.

The Text Types of School

A number of written genres associated with learning in school have been identified by a group of linguists working in Sydney, including, among many others, Jim Martin, Joan Rothery, Frances Christie, Beverley Derewianka, and Jenny Hammond. These genres include recounts, narratives, reports, procedures, arguments, discussions, and explanations. (For a detailed description of these, see Derewianka 1990.) In this book I will use the term *text types* to refer specifically to these genres, in order to differentiate them from the wider range of genres used outside school. One of the commonest text types that children are expected to use early on in their school life (and, ironically, probably one of the most complex) is the narrative. Let's look at some of its specific characteristics.

Narratives, like all text types, have a *purpose*, which may be to entertain or perhaps to teach (as fables do). They also have a *particular organizational structure*, which is most typically displayed in traditional stories. First, there is an *orientation*, the purpose of which is to set the scene, introduce the characters, and say when and where the narrative is set. Then there are a number of *events*, which lead to some kind of problem, sometimes referred to as a *complication*. Finally, the problem is resolved in the final part of the story, the *resolution*. Figure 4–1 contains a very shortened version of the story of Jack and Beanstalk, which illustrates how each of these stages is integral to the story.

Once upon a time there was a boy named Jack, who lived with his mother in a small village. They were very poor and their only possession was a cow, which gave them milk, and an old axe, which hung on the wall of their house.	Orientation: *sets the scene, gives details of who, when, where.*
One day his mother said to Jack, "We are so poor that we must sell the cow. You must take it to market and sell it to buy food." So Jack took the cow and set off to market. On his way there he met an old man who offered to exchange Jack's cow for some beans. Jack said, "My mother will be very angry with me if I don't take back money. We need to buy food." "Don't worry," replied the old man. "These are no ordinary beans. They are magic beans, and they will bring you good luck!" Jack felt sorry for the old man, for he looked even poorer than Jack, and so he agreed to exchange the cow for the magic beans. "You are a kind boy," said the old man, "and you will be well rewarded." When he got home and told his mother what he had done, she was very angry.	Events: *relates a number of events in sequence.*

FIGURE 4–1. *Organizational Structure of a Narrative*

(continued)

"You stupid boy," she shouted. "You have sold our most valuable possession for a handful of beans." And she threw the beans out of the window. The next day, when Jack woke up, there, in the garden, where his mother had thrown the beans, was a huge beanstalk. It was as thick as a tree and so tall it seemed to go right up into the sky. Jack stared and stared at the beanstalk, and remembered the old man's words. Taking his axe, he began to climb up the beanstalk. Up and up he climbed. For many hours he kept climbing until, at last, he could see the top of the beanstalk. Right at the top of the beanstalk, asleep on the ground, was a huge, ugly giant. And in front of him lay a heap of treasure. There were gold and silver coins, and piles of precious jewels. Very quietly, so as not to wake the giant, Jack started to fill his coat pockets with the giant's treasure.	
Just as Jack had taken all he could carry, the giant opened one eye and saw Jack. "Who are you?" he roared. He opened the other eye, and then he stood up. Jack could hardly see his head it was so far away. He turned and ran and started to climb down the beanstalk as fast as he could. The giant strode after him, and Jack felt sure he was about to die!	Complication: *states the problem.*
But as the giant was about to reach down and grab Jack, Jack remembered the axe. He swung it backwards and then, as hard as he could, he chopped into the beanstalk just above his head. Again and again he chopped until, at last, the top of the beanstalk crashed down out of the sky, carrying the giant with it. With a loud roar he disappeared and fell to earth. And Jack climbed safely down the beanstalk carrying enough jewels to look after his mother and himself for the rest of his life.	Resolution: *relates how the problem is solved.*

FIGURE 4–1. *Organizational Structure of a Narrative (continued)*

There are also typical *linguistic features* common to narratives:

- They are sequenced in time, and this is often signaled by the conjunctions or connectives that are used. In the beanstalk story, the time connectives that sequence events include *once upon a time, one day, when, the next day, for many hours, at last, and.*

- They usually use the past tense.
- They use many "action" verbs that describe what people do. In the beanstalk story, the action verbs include *took, met, threw, woke, climbed, stood, turned, ran, strode, chopped, swung, crashed, disappeared*.
- They often contain dialogue, and so they also contain "saying" verbs that explain how people speak: *said, replied, shouted, roared*.

If you compare the beanstalk narrative above to another text type, such as a set of written instructions, it is clear that each type is distinctive: they have different purposes, a different overall structure, different ways of organizing or linking ideas, and different linguistic features. For teacher reference, the key features of some of the major text types of school are summarized in Figure 4–2, under the headings *purpose, organizational structure, connectives (linking words)*, and *other language features*. As the next part of the chapter will demonstrate, being aware of the most important linguistic features of some of the text types of school will help you make these explicit to students, and will help guide your assessment. Note though that these linguistic features are not intended to be passed directly onto students as they stand: a later section of this chapter discusses a suggested process for developing a range of text types with learners.

Explicit Teaching About Writing

There is considerable debate at the current time around the notion of "explicit" teaching. This implies a very different approach to the teaching of writing than that embodied in progressive "process" approaches of the 1970s and 1980s.

Process approaches, unlike the more traditional approaches that preceded them, put the learner at the center of the learning process. In relation to writing, the major themes within this approach are that children learn to write most effectively when they are encouraged to start with their own expressive language, that "meaning" is more important than "form," and that writing should take place frequently and within a context that provides "real" audiences for writing (see, for example Graves 1983; Cambourne 1988). A particular feature of this approach is the importance placed on the processes of learning. An underlying assumption in many classrooms has been that, given the right classroom environment and a climate that expects a quantity of writing across a range of purposes and forms, children will automatically learn to write on a variety of subjects and in many forms, just as they learned to speak without formal instruction.

While the move away from the traditional teacher-centered classroom has been generally welcomed, there have been a number of critiques of progressive approaches, particularly in relation to minority students or those less familiar with the language of school. Many ESL teachers in particular have argued for more formal instruction in the structures of language and the conventions of writing. While acknowledging the strengths of the progressive movement in developing approaches that recognize the

Type of text	Recount	Narrative (story)	Report	Procedure	Discussion
	What I did at the weekend	The elephant and the mouse	Insects	How to make a healthy meal	(one side) Argument (two sides) (e.g., Should smoking be made illegal?)
Purpose	To tell what happened	To entertain, to teach	To give information	To tell how to do something	To persuade others, to take a position and justify it
Organization	Orientation (tells who, where, when) Series of events Personal comment/conclusion	Orientation (tells who, where, when) Series of events Problem Resolution	General statement Characteristic (e.g., habitat) Characteristic (e.g., appearance) Characteristic (e.g., food, etc.) May have subheadings	Goal Steps in sequence	Personal statement of position Argument(s) and supporting evidence Possibly counter-argument(s) and supporting evidence Conclusion
Connectives (Linking words)	To do with time (first, then, next, afterwards, at the end of the day)	To do with time (one day, once upon a time, later, afterwards, in the end)	Not usually used	first, second, third, finally, etc.	first, second, in addition, therefore, however, on the other hand
Other language features	Past tense, tells about what happened Describing words	Past tense, tells about what happened Action verbs Describing words May have dialogue and verbs of "saying"	Uses "to be" and "to have" (e.g., A fly is an insect. It has six legs.) Special vocabulary	Uses verbs to give instructions (e.g., take, mix, add, chop, bake, etc.)	May use persuasive language (e.g., it is obviously wrong, it is clearly stupid that ...)

FIGURE 4–2. *Some Text Types of School*

importance of interesting and interactive educational settings, it has been argued that such approaches also tend to reinforce existing social inequities, since what is expected of learners is often not made explicit (Martin 1986, 1989; Martin, Christie, and Rothery 1987; Delpit 1988; Boomer 1989). Susan Feez (1985), writing about the Australian context, has argued:

> in many respects . . . progressive approaches have reinforced the inequalities of access which are characteristic of older, traditional pedagogies. It is simply that in progressive pedagogies, the way these inequalities are perpetuated becomes invisible. Learners' individuality and freedom may be more highly valued in progressive classrooms, but during and at the end of their courses of study learners are still assessed against the standards of the dominant culture . . . although classrooms are more pleasant, what is actually expected of learners in order for them to be successful is not made explicit . . . progressive classrooms tend to reinforce existing social inequalities of opportunity because it seems that it is the learner rather than the educational institution, who is to be blamed for failure in such benevolent and rich learning environments. (9)

Lisa Delpit (1988), writing in the context of the education of African American students in the United States, has also argued that the conventions of writing must be explicitly taught, and that they will not simply be picked up by students for whom the language and assumptions of the school are unfamiliar. As she argues, if you are not already a participant in the dominant culture, being told explicitly the rules of that culture makes acquiring power easier. As Delpit notes, entering a new culture is easier, both psychologically and pragmatically, if information about the appropriateness of behavior is made explicit to those outside the culture, rather than conveyed as implicit codes, as it would be to those who are members of the community by birth. Delpit concludes, "Unless one has the leisure of a lifetime of immersion to learn them, explicit presentation makes learning immeasurably easier" (283). She explains:

> Some children come to school with more accoutrements of the culture of power already in place—"cultural capital" as some critical theorists refer to it—some with less. Many liberal educators hold that the primary goal for education is for children to become autonomous, to develop fully while they are in the classroom setting without having arbitrary, outside standards forced upon them. This is a very reasonable goal for people whose children are already participants in the culture of power and who have internalized its codes. But parents who don't function within that culture often want something else. It's not that they disagree with the former aim, it's just that they want something more. They want to ensure that the school provides their children with discourse patterns, interactional styles, and spoken and written language codes that will allow them success in the larger society. (285)

Delpit, like Feez, suggests that where educational standards are not accorded a high priority for minority students, then—no matter how friendly, egalitarian, and caring the environment—classrooms may still work against students, even though in a benign and less obvious way. While some teachers may feel uncomfortable about teaching in a way that seems to exhibit their power in the classroom, this very lack of explicitness, whether it is about rules of conduct or forms of writing, may actually prevent some students from achieving educational success. One clear implication of this argument is that the educational curriculum must include explicit teaching of those forms of language that will enable students to succeed in school and actively participate in the dominant community.

Thus, whereas progressive theorists have argued for an understanding of writing through a focus on personal growth and process, proponents of explicit teaching have argued for an understanding of the linguistic nature of texts as they are produced within social contexts and for various purposes. Further, they argue that educators have a responsibility to intervene in the learning process (Martin, Christie, and Rothery 1987; Kalantzis, Cope, Noble, and Poynting 1991).

So what does it mean to teach "explicitly"? Let's begin with what it *doesn't* mean! It doesn't mean a return to the teaching of traditional grammar, and to meaningless drills and exercises devoid of functional and communicative purpose. Nor does it mean that "grammar" is taught separately from the authentic use of language. Neither does it mean a breaking up of language into its component parts of speech, or a fragmentation of the timetable into spelling, dictation, composition, and so on, or a separation of the macro-skills of reading, writing, listening, and speaking. It *does* mean that students are encouraged to reflect on how language is used for a range of purposes and with a range of audiences, and that teachers focus explicitly on those aspects of language that enable students to do this. Explicit teaching is related to real-life use, so that understanding *about* language is developed in the context of actual language use. It aims to foster active involvement in learning, independence in writing, and the ability to critique the ways that language is used in authentic contexts, such as the ways it is used to persuade and control.

The Curriculum Cycle

Let's turn now to what these principles might look like in the classroom. Derewianka (1990) and others involved in the "genre" movement in Australia have identified four stages (named the Curriculum Cycle) through which a particular text type can be made explicit to students. These four stages of the Curriculum Cycle have come to be known as *building up the field*, *modeling the text type*, *joint construction*, and *independent writing*. Each of these stages has a particular teaching purpose:

- *Stage 1: Building the Field.* In this stage the aim is to make sure that your students have enough background knowledge of the topic to be able to write about it. The focus here is primarily on the content or information of the text. At this stage, children are a long way from writing a text themselves, and activities will involve speaking, listening, reading, information gathering, note taking, and reading.

- *Stage 2: Modeling the Text Type.* In this stage the aim is for students to become familiar with the purpose, overall structure, and linguistic features of the type of text they are going to write. The focus here is therefore on the form and function of the particular text type that the students are going to write.
- *Stage 3: Joint Construction.* Here the teacher and students write a text together, so that students can see how the text is written. The focus here is on illustrating the process of writing a text, considering both the content and the language.
- *Stage 4: Independent Writing.* At this stage students write their own text.

It's important to recognize that this Curriculum Cycle may take several weeks or longer to go through and may be the overall framework for an entire topic. It is not a single lesson!

Here are some classroom activities that you might find useful for each of the stages. Not all activities will be appropriate for all ages, and they also are not all appropriate for use in the teaching of every text type. In addition, from your general teaching experience you can no doubt think of other language-focused activities and ways of developing the topic. However, the activities suggested here illustrate how this approach to writing integrates speaking, listening, reading, and writing, and integrates language with curriculum content.

As an example, let's imagine that you want to help children write a report—that is, a factual account of what something is (or was) like. First, you need to make a decision about what curriculum topic would require students to write a report. (In this case, let's say dinosaurs.) Always be sure to consider what you have already planned to teach (in any curriculum area). It's important that the Curriculum Cycle should be based on your regular curriculum—it shouldn't be seen as an "add-on" to what you would normally be teaching.

Stage 1: Building Knowledge of the Topic

The aim here is to build up background knowledge, and so the focus is primarily on the "content" of the topic. Since the primary purpose of this stage is to collect information, some of the activities could be carried out by groups of students in their mother tongue, although they will need to use English to share the information with others. A useful form of classroom organization for a number of the activities discussed here is an **expert/home grouping,** described in Chapter 2. This kind of organization involves note-taking, listening, speaking, and reading, and it provides a genuine need for authentic communication. While collaborative learning strategies are important for all children, they offer to ESL children a range of situations in which they are exposed to and learn to use subject-specific language.

Again, the **expert/home grouping** strategy for collaborative learning depends on groups of children holding different information from others in the class. You can vary how you do this, but as a general principle, different groups of students become "expert" in a different aspect of the topic during a particular activity. In this example, groups of four to six could choose to carry out research on a particular dinosaur. Once they have become "experts," the students regroup so that the home group contains one student from each of the "expert" groups. The experts' job is to share what they have learned with the rest of the group.

Here are some ways to build up a shared knowledge of the topic. They are in no particular order but are simply examples of activities that you could use. As you can see, an important aspect of this stage is that it involves a lot of speaking, listening, and reading, and develops a range of research skills.

- Build up **a semantic web** of students' current knowledge of the topic, teaching new vocabulary as appropriate.
- Use **wallpapering** to collect ideas based on students' current knowledge.
- Gather a list of questions from the children of things they would like to find out about (e.g., *why did the dinosaurs disappear?*). For beginner ESL students, this also models the structure of question forms.
- Read about the topic with students using shared reading or big books. This could include both nonfiction and fiction texts. If you use both kinds, there is an opportunity to discuss with students the different purposes of each. With a narrative text you could also talk about what is fact and what is fiction, and ask children what facts (if any) they have learned about dinosaurs from the story.
- Use pictures to elicit or teach vocabulary. You could also get students to match labels to simple line drawings, introducing more technical vocabulary such as *horns, jaws, curved teeth, crest, spine, thumb claw, scaly skin, tail, plates, spikes*.
- Develop a **word wall/word bank** about the topic, where technical vocabulary can be displayed.
- Use **jigsaw listening** to extend the children's knowledge base. Each group could listen to audiotaped information about a different dinosaur, or a different theory about why they disappeared. They could make notes and later share the information with the rest of the class, either in groups or with the whole class.
- Use technological resources (the Internet is a wonderful resource for many topics) to access additional information. Here is a context where you could again use a home/expert grouping.
- Get the students to **interview** an expert in the field. They could write a letter inviting an expert into the classroom and prepare questions to ask.
- Use a **picture and sentence matching** game. Get younger or beginning ESL children to match pictures and sentences about dinosaurs (e.g., *Stegosaurus had a row of plates on its back* and *Diplodocus was the longest of all the dinosaurs*). You could turn this into a barrier game whereby Student A reads out a sentence— *It has a row of plates on its back*—and Student B points to the appropriate picture.

- Use **barrier games** such as Find the Difference to describe the appearance of dinosaurs, such as by finding the differences between Stegosaurus and Triceratops. (See Figure 4–3.)
- Use the topic to develop library skills by visiting the library and getting the students to suggest where they might find the specific information they are looking for.

A

B

FIGURE 4–3.   *Find the Differences Between the Dinosaurs*

- Watch a video and provide an **information grid** for pairs of children to complete as they watch. Or you could use two sets of questions, with one half of the class answering one set, in pairs, and the other half answering the other set, in pairs. Later, pairs from each half could form groups of four and share their information.
- Visit a museum and give different groups of children different questions to research. Children would later share information in the expert/home groups as mentioned earlier.
- As an ongoing activity during this stage, build up an **information grid** with the class that summarizes the information the students have gathered. This could be formed on a large sheet of paper and displayed on the wall. This is a "working document," not an end in itself, so both you and the students can add to it as they discover more information. Encourage children to do this whenever they learn something new. Alternatively, children can also develop their own information grids, individually, in pairs, or in a group. In the following stages, these information summaries will be very important.
- Use the topic to practice or introduce grammar structures that are particularly meaningful to the topic. For example, although scientists know a great deal about dinosaurs, there is much that is still speculative. We don't know for sure why dinosaurs became extinct, nor why they grew so large. Very recent evidence suggests that they may have been warm-blooded. It is important for learners to be able to express these uncertainties, and this would be a meaningful context in which to introduce or remind students about how to use modality, the way in which speakers express degrees of likelihood or probability (e.g., *may be, perhaps, might, could be*), or degrees of usuality (e.g., *sometimes, often, frequently*). Ways of expressing probability could form a word bank (e.g., *might have been, may have been, possibly, probably, perhaps, it is possible that*) from which students can construct sentences:

> *Perhaps dinosaurs disappeared because the climate changed.*
> *Dinosaurs might have disappeared because the climate changed.*
> *They probably communicated with their eyes and the sounds they made.*
> *They may have been warm-blooded.*

Stage 2: Modeling the Text

This stage aims to build up students' understandings of the purpose, overall structure, and language features of the particular text type the class is focusing on. You should choose a text that is similar to the one you will use in the next stage (joint construction) and to the one that students will eventually write themselves. Model texts may be commercially produced, teacher-written, or texts written previously by other students. It is helpful to have this model text on an overhead or a large sheet of paper, so that you can talk about it as a class more easily. For our example, you would choose a short report about dinosaurs, or about a particular dinosaur.

During this stage, introduce some meta-language—language to talk about language—to the students as it is needed. Words like *connectives, organizational structure, text type, verbs,* and *tense* will make it easier for you to talk about the key features, and for the students to self-evaluate their own texts later. Contrary to much debate about the place of the teaching of "grammar," research in Australia has shown that students do not have difficulty in understanding these concepts, and that providing a label helps make explicit key aspects of writing (Williams 1999). The principle here, of course, is that these grammatical terms are taught *in the context of language use.* Here are some steps to follow.

- Read and show the model report to the students, and discuss with them its purpose—to present factual information on a topic. (If students are already familiar with narratives, you could discuss with them the difference between the purposes of a narrative and of a report.)
- Draw attention to the organizational structure or "shape" of the text, and the function of each stage (e.g., reports begin with a general statement, the purpose of which is to locate what is being talked about in the broader scheme of things, and the rest of the report consists of facts about various aspects of the subject). Then focus on any grammatical structures and vocabulary that are important in the text. You may want to focus on modality, as discussed earlier, or on the verbs *be* and *have,* since these are very common in information reports. (Note, however, that here they will be used in the past tense since we are referring to things no longer in existence.) Alternatively, you might prefer to let the students themselves decide on these features, in which case you will need to provide careful guidance and questioning, and the students will probably need to examine several examples of the same text type.
- Students in pairs do a **text reconstruction** of part of the report, where they sequence jumbled sentences into a coherent text. Alternately, you could mix up the sentences from two reports so that students must first sort out which sentence belongs to which report, and then sequence them.
- Use a **dictogloss** to provide another model of the text type. The content of this should be taken from the current topic (e.g., you could choose a text that describes one of the dinosaurs the children are researching). In turn, this will also be a source of further information.
- Use the model text as a **cloze** exercise, making the "gaps" according to the grammatical features or vocabulary you are focusing on. Children will also enjoy using a **monster cloze** or a **vanishing cloze**.
- Use part of the model text as a **running dictation**.
- Once the students have a clear idea of the characteristics of a report (or whatever text type you are focusing on), remind them of these characteristics and

write them up as a chart that can be displayed on the wall. (Figure 4–2 may be useful as teacher reference here, but note that this diagram is not intended for direct student use.)

Stage 3: Joint Construction

At this stage, students are ready to think about writing, although they will not yet be writing alone. The teacher or students decide on the topic they will write about, but again it should be an example of the same text type, such as a report on one type of dinosaur. To ensure that students have sufficient background knowledge, encourage them to draw on the information grid the class developed in Stage 1.

It will help you to understand the teaching purpose of this stage if you return to Chapter 1 and the example of Nigel talking with his parents. There we saw how the story Nigel told was jointly constructed—while the *meanings* were initiated by Nigel, his parents helped with the *wording*. This is a natural process, and for most adults an intuitive one. The joint construction stage of writing mirrors the same process. The students give suggestions and contribute ideas while the teacher scribes, and together the teacher and students discuss how the writing can be improved. Throughout the process, the teacher and students constantly reread together what they have written, with the teacher asking questions like these:

> *What do we need to start with?*
> *Is that the best way to say it?*
> *Can anyone think of a better word than that?*
> *Is this all OK now? Can anyone see anything that needs fixing up?*

You should also remind students of the model texts they have looked at. For example, ask questions such as:

> *Can you remember what the other reports were like?*
> *What do you think we should talk about next?*

At this stage, teacher and students together discuss the overall structure of the text, suggest more appropriate vocabulary, consider alternative ways of wording an idea, and work on correcting grammatical mistakes, spelling, and punctuation. This is a time when there can be an explicit focus on grammar, but, unlike the traditional classroom, it occurs in functionally relevant ways—in the context of actual language use, and at the point of need.

In the following excerpt, which is taken from a joint construction of an explanation about how a telephone works, two students below talk about language. The excerpt shows evidence of quite sophisticated understandings about using reference words.

> *We keep repeating "the exchange," "the exchange," "the exchange."*

Let's put "it" instead.
But they won't know what "it" is!
Yes they will 'cause we've already said it. (from Derewianka 1990, 59)

At the joint construction stage, then, the teacher encourages students to focus on all aspects of writing. But this stage should also model the process of writing: as suggestions are made, the teacher will cross out, amend, and add words. Once this first draft is complete, the teacher or a student can rewrite it on a large sheet of paper, and it can remain in the classroom as an additional model text.

While the joint construction stage is teacher-guided, it should not be seen as teacher-dominated. The teacher does not simply write her "own" text. Rather, her role is to take up the ideas of the students, leading the discussion of any linguistic aspects of the text that students are still learning to control. This is a very important part of the curriculum cycle because it illustrates to students both the *process* of composing text, and a *product* that is similar to what they will later write themselves.

Stage 4: Independent Writing

This is the final stage of the cycle, when students write their own texts. They can do this writing individually or in pairs. For our example, they could choose a dinosaur to write about (but not the same one as used in Stages 2 and 3). By now there has been a considerable amount of scaffolding for the writing. Students have developed considerable background knowledge about the subject, are aware of the linguistic characteristics of the text type, and have jointly constructed a similar text. This preparation, or scaffolding, for writing will help ensure that they have the knowledge and skills to be able to write their own texts with confidence.

As students write, remind them about the process of writing: doing a first draft, self-editing, discussing the draft with friends and later with the teacher, and finally producing a "published" text. The published texts can be displayed in the classroom or made into a class book. If you photocopy a few of the students' texts (with their permission), they will also serve as useful models and resources for other classes.

A Scaffolding Approach to Writing

It is easy to see how the notion of scaffolding applies to this kind of teaching. At no stage are learners expected to carry out alone a task with which they are not familiar, yet at the same time they are constantly being "stretched" in their language development and expected to take responsibility for those tasks they are capable of doing alone. At each stage there is systematic guidance and support until learners are able to carry out the writing task for themselves. Consider how different this approach is to the traditional one-off writing task, when students were expected to write a single and final copy at one sitting, or some "process" approaches in which students were expected to make their own choices about writing topic and how to approach it. While imagination and ownership are important concepts in teaching writing, they are insufficient to ensure that all students, especially those less familiar with the language of school, will learn to write in a broad range of contexts.

Using the Curriculum Cycle

The cycle will take you some time to complete. However, in the case of reports, for example, not only will students learn how to write a report, but they will also learn a lot about the topic (and thus develop particular knowledge in a curriculum area). As well, they will practice the study skills of note taking and of locating, summarizing, and reinterpreting information. The cycle includes plenty of opportunities for reading, listening, and speaking, and you may decide to integrate it with focused teaching of these skills. In addition, students will learn how to write, edit, and evaluate any similar text that they might need to write at another time.

Of course, students will not know all there is to know about this text type after the first use of the cycle. It should be repeated throughout the year, using appropriately chosen material for the age of the students. However, as they become more familiar with the particular text type, it probably won't be necessary to continue to go through Stages 2 and 3 in quite such detail.

It has sometimes been suggested that the cycle simply presents different text types as a series of "recipes" that students are then expected to follow slavishly. Creativity and the writer's voice, it is argued, will be stifled. However, making rules and expectations explicit to students does not limit their freedom and autonomy. On the contrary, it gives them the tools to be creative and autonomous. Once students are aware of the conventions of any of the text types, they will be able to manipulate them for their own purposes.

Good short story writers, for example, often don't follow the overall structure discussed earlier. They may begin with the resolution and narrate the story as a series of flashbacks, or manipulate the sequence in a whole range of other ways. But it would be foolish to suggest that good writers are unaware of traditional narrative writing; indeed, it is precisely this awareness that allows them to exploit and manipulate their writing in new ways, and to make conscious choices about how they write. We need to reflect this in the classroom. If students are to have real choices about what and how they write, they need to be shown what the range of options is. Otherwise, they may simply remain with what they know, writing about a limited range of things in the same way. And it is important to remember that the "rules" and conventions that govern different types of writing have not been imposed by linguists, but simply describe what these text types look like in the real world.

Scaffolding for Young Writers

You may feel that the discussion so far is more relevant to older students or those more advanced in English. However, the same approach can be used with very young students and those new to English, although the length of the text will be much shorter. One of the simplest text types to begin with is a personal recount. A recount reconstructs past experience, and is a retelling of an activity or a sequence of events in which the speaker or writer has been involved. A school excursion provides an ideal context for developing recounts. For example, on the day of an excursion with her second graders to visit a local dam and the surrounding countryside, one teacher brought a camera and took photographs of the day. The children took field notes and made sketches of what they saw. When they returned to school, they shared their observations in the form of oral recounts. Later they relived the excursion through the photographs, and as each photo was discussed, the teacher helped the children talk about what they had done, using the sequence of photographs as prompts of the day's events: *we left school early in the morning*; *we got on the bus*; *we visited the national park*; *we had our lunch*; *we visited the dam*; and so on. After the oral discussion, the sequence of photographs served as a prompt for the children's own writing.

Many young writers rely on *and then* for sequencing recounts and narratives, so in this class the teacher decided to model a broader range of connectives (*later, next, afterwards, finally* . . .). Students helped build up a **word bank** of these to draw on in their own writing. (They can continue to add to word banks as they think of similar examples themselves or come across them in their reading.) As Chapter 1 pointed out, as far as possible teachers should try to have the range of learners in their class complete the same or similar tasks—what will vary is the kind and degree of the scaffolding teachers provide. For children at the early stages of writing in English, provide more support, such as a simple organizational framework and some suggested connecting words. You could also provide a list of some of the vocabulary they will need to use. Here's an example:

On _____ our class went to_____ .
First we visited _____. We saw_____ there.
Then we went to _____.
Next we visited _____ and saw _____.
Afterwards we went to _____ and saw _____.
Finally we got back on the bus and _____.
We got back to school at _____. It was fun!

Scaffolding for Children New to English

There are many other ways of scaffolding writing for learners very new to English. Here are some other general ideas.

- Actively encourage writing in the first language. This reduces some of the frustration children often feel when they are unable to participate in classroom tasks that they are well able to carry out in their mother tongue. If possible, provide a translation on a facing page (perhaps with the help of a parent). Having a bilingual account will not only help learners understand the English version, but allow them to display their literacy skills, which may be considerable. In addition, bilingual texts allow native English-speaking children to see that English is not the only language in which people can communicate.

- For a recount or a narrative, have learners draw a sequence of events or **story map** and dictate what they want to say. Write this text for them, which they can trace over or copy.
- Use **picture sequencing** with a group of students as a basis for a simple narrative.
- Have learners match photos or pictures to simple sentences or labels, or use a **barrier game** for picture and sentence matching like the one described in Stage 1 earlier.
- Use **dialogue journals** between yourself and the ESL learner, or between the ESL learner and an English-speaking buddy. These are ongoing written conversations where each partner writes a single short sentence responding to the other.
- Make **jumbled sentences**. Get learners to tell you a sentence about themselves, something they have done, or something they like. Scribe it for them and then get them to cut this up into single words. Learners rearrange the jumbled sentence, read it, and then rewrite it. If they are literate in their mother tongue, get them to write an equivalent sentence in their mother tongue too.
- A variation on **jumbled sentences** is to write the same sentence on two strips of card. Cut one into the individual words. Students place the matching word on top of the uncut strip. This is useful for drawing attention to the shape of words and to the way they are spelled.
- For learners who are not completely new to English, but who still need strong support, provide them with an explicit framework for the kind of writing the class is doing. This kind of explicit scaffolding means that students are able to take part in the same tasks as the rest of the class—as Chapter 1 pointed out, it is the nature of the scaffolding, rather than the task itself, that changes. Figure 4–4 is an example of how a fairly complex text type—a discussion—can be scaffolded in this way.

Assessing Students' Writing: What Their Texts Can Tell Us

There are a range of reasons for assessment. Among the most important of these is the ongoing assessment teachers carry out to find out what their students are able to do. Only if we know students' current abilities can subsequent teaching be truly responsive, and only then can we plan how to take students further. Put another way, and using the Vygotskian idea of the zone of proximal development discussed in Chapter 1, we must know what the learner is able to do alone before we know what to scaffold next. This kind of assessment is not an extra item for which you must find additional time; it can occur during any normal classroom teaching. Here is a suggestion about how to analyze

Title: _____

What the discussion is about, and my opinion

The topic of this discussion is . . .

My opinion is that . . .

Arguments for

There are a number of reasons why I believe this.

1. First

2. In addition

3. Finally

Counterarguments (arguments against)

1. On the other hand, some people argue

2. In addition

3. They also say

Conclusion

However, my view is that . . .

because . . .

FIGURE 4–4. *Discussion Framework (for students needing more scaffolding)*

students' writing to find out both what they are able to achieve and the areas in which they need help. To do this you will need to look at a piece that represents what the writer can do alone. It need not be their first draft, but it should not yet have been discussed in a conference.

Here are two examples of narrative writing, both from ESL students. The first comes from a student who is still in the early stages of English, and the second comes from a younger child who is already fluent in spoken English. Take a moment to think about what each writer knows, and what kind of help they need.

Text 1: turtle and wolf

One day the turtle out the river to find the food.

He go went the sun.

The sun very hot the turtle he want go back.

The turtle crying because he can't go back. the wolf thought the turtle he think turtle was singing. The wolf said "you don't singing to me I put you on the sun," "Don't worry I can get into my shell. "I threw you to the river.

"Don't do that."

The wolf threw turtle to the river. The turtle said "thank old mr wolf.

Text 2: Night

One night I was walking throgth the woods I heard something strange I didn't know what it was I looked I still didn't know what it was I looking it was an owl he led me to house he knocked on the door a which answer come little boy I might turn you into a frog all my prisoners are hiding somewhere so you can't escape if you try to they will catch you so I will turn you into a which their are stairs but their are prisoners hiding you can'not go up their because they have the stuf to turn you into a frog so I wouldn't try it she let me go I ran home as fast as I could I was home at last what happen I will tell you in the morning then I went to bed.

What were your first reactions to the two texts? If you were to look only at sentence grammar, you would probably be more critical of Text 1 than of Text 2. Text 1 has many more grammatical mistakes, particularly in the use of verbs, and it is quite clearly written by a second language learner. Text 2, despite the fact that it is written with minimal punctuation, has a much closer control of standard grammar. However, you may also feel that Text 1 is a more coherent piece: we can follow the story line, and this is much harder to follow in Text 2.

Before you read further, look again at the discussion of the features of a narrative discussed at the beginning of this chapter, and in Figure 4–2. Then consider the texts again, this time thinking about the question framework in Figure 4–5 as you read.

These questions are designed to help you think in a systematic way about what you are reading, and about what the student knows and can do, as well as to highlight future

1. General Comments	2. Text Type	3. Overall Organization	4. Cohesion	5. Vocabulary	6. Sentence Grammar	7. Spelling
Is the overall meaning clear?	What kind of text is this?	Is the overall structural organization appropriate to the text type?	Are the ideas linked with the appropriate connectives? *(note that these will vary with the text type, see Chapter 4)*	Is appropriate vocabulary used?	Is this accurate (e.g., subject-verb agreements, correct use of tenses, correct use of word order, etc.)?	Is this accurate?
Are the main ideas developed?	Is this appropriate for the writer's purpose?	Are any stages missing?		Is there semantic variety (e.g., does the writer use a range of words for "big"; *huge, massive, large, gigantic, etc.*)? *(note that semantic variety will be appropriate for narratives and recounts, but probably not for more factual texts, such as reports and instructions)*		If the writer does not yet produce correct spelling, what does the writer know about spelling (e.g., evidence of sound-symbol correspondence)?
Does the writing reflect the writer's other classroom language experiences (e.g., what they have read or talked about)?	Has the writer written this text type before?		Is there an appropriate variety of these connectives?			
What is your overall impression compared to other things the learner has written?			Are pronouns used correctly (e.g., *he* and *she*)?			
			Do pronouns have a clear referent (e.g., is it clear what words like *he, she, this, there,* etc. are referring to)?			

FIGURE 4–5. *Question Framework for Assessing Writing*

learning needs. The framework takes a holistic and top-down view of writing, focusing first on the overall meaning, then on the overall organization, the ways that sentences are connected, sentence construction, and finally spelling and punctuation. Leaving spelling and punctuation until last is not to suggest they are not important, simply that correcting the spelling of a poor piece of writing results in a correctly spelled poor piece of writing—the piece of writing itself is not substantially improved! When helping students with their writing, spelling and punctuation must be considered in the final version, but only after other more fundamental aspects of writing have been thought about first.

Your responses to these sets of questions may have given you a quite different perspective on the two texts. For Text 1, you will probably have responded positively to Questions 1, 2, and 3, and to some degree to 4. Your response to 5 and 7 will also probably have been quite positive. It is only when we look at 6 that difficulties are evident. So think about what that student *can* do, and what he knows about writing (and how much of his ability to write would go unnoticed if sentence grammar were the sole focus of the assessment). By contrast, Text 2 is actually much less comprehensible or coherent, and compared to your assessment of Text 1, you probably found it in several ways a far less successful text.

If you simplify and adapt the question framework, you can also share it with your students, and demonstrate how they might use it to reflect, proofread, and evaluate their own writing. Very often when asked to edit their writing, students focus almost exclusively on spelling and punctuation because they are unaware of what else to look at. Encouraging students to think more holistically about their writing will mean building up a shared meta-language—for example, using terms such as *text type*, *overall structure*, and *connectives*. These can be introduced gradually and in context, and will help students build up a language to talk about language, as well as draw their attention to significant aspects of their writing.

An example of how the framework might be filled in for the writer of the first text is included in Figure 4–6. A framework like this will help you keep an ongoing profile of individual students' writing development. Try to jot down comments as you are conferencing with students or reading their texts. Even if these notes are brief, they will help you build up a clear idea of what kinds of texts your students are able to control, and any linguistic difficulties they may be having. One teacher with whom I worked developed a system of color-coding, using one color for indicating positive achievements and another indicating the area where future teaching was needed.

An alternative way of using the framework is to use it to build up a *class profile*. To assess how well a group of students is able to use a particular text type, write the names of the students down the left-hand side and comment briefly on each one. You will then be able to see what abilities and difficulties they have in common.

Although this kind of assessment is time-consuming, you will find that you get faster the more you use it. It is also time well spent, because in reflecting on students' writing in this way, you are able to better target your future teaching to specific student needs. In doing this you are also "individualizing" the program. This does not

1. General Comments	2. Text Type	3. Overall Organization	4. Cohesion	5. Vocabulary	6. Sentence Grammar	7. Spelling and Punctuation
Meaning clear and all elements of story present	Narrative	Good—has orientation events problem resolut on	Used reference correctly throughout	Good Used vocab. from the story	Needs help with the past tense Introduce more "saying verbs," like answered, replied, begged ...	Spelling good Needs help with setting out of dialogue

FIGURE 4–6. *Assessment of Text 1*

mean developing an individual program for every student, which for most busy teachers is a practical impossibility, but it does mean that the classroom program will be as responsive as possible to the individual needs indicated by the profile. Finally, the profile will indicate what students *can* achieve (as we saw in Text 1) as well as where they have difficulties, and will be a useful basis for giving feedback to the students themselves, to parents, and to other teachers.

In Summary

Here is one final comment about the approach to writing taken in this chapter. The more time you have spent on the stages of the Curriculum Cycle, and the more planned and responsive the scaffolding, the more likely it is that students will write effectively, feel they have control over what they are writing, and gain confidence in using written language. Both you and your students will feel proud of their achievements. It is certainly preferable to spending endless time correcting mistakes in students' writing because they have not had sufficient support earlier in the process.

Suggestions for Further Reading

DEREWIANKA, B. 1990. *Exploring How Texts Work*. Portsmouth, NH: Heinemann.

MARTIN, J. 1990. "Literacy in Science: Learning to Handle Literacy as Technology." In *Literacy for a Changing World*, ed. F. Christie. Hawthorn, Victoria, AU: ACER.

ROTHERY, J. 1992. "Assessing Children's Writing." In *Language Assessment in Primary Classrooms*, ed. B. Derewianka. London: Harcourt Brace Jovanovich.

5

Reading in a Second Language

Literacy in a second language develops as in the first—
globally, not linearly, and in a variety of rich contexts.
Rigg and Allen, *When They Don't All Speak English:*
Integrating the ESL Student in the Regular Classroom

Contributions to Reading Theory

As suggested by the following introduction—which proved very difficult to type and
has caused my spell checker to light up the computer screen!—the approach taken in
this chapter is that effective readers do a range of things simultaneously:

Thr hs bn a lt of dbat ovr th pst tn yrs abt th tchng of rding. Sme see rding as th mastry of phncs,
othrs as a procss of prdctn whrby the rdcr uss bckgrnd knwldge and knwledge of th lngge systm
to prdict mning.

    Thees diffreing veiws haev infelunced the wya raeding has bene tuahgt. Appraochse haev
vareid betwene thoes who argeu that the taeching of phoincs is the msot imprtoant elmeent of
a raeding prorgam, and thoes who argeu fro a whoel-language appraohc in whchi childnre laern
to raed by perdicting maenngi.

    But it shou_ be obvi_ to anyo_ readi_ thi_ th_ goo_ read_ use a rang_ of strateg_ to
gai_ mean_ fro_ writ_ tex_.

You were probably able to read these first three paragraphs quite easily, even
though they may have looked quite strange. Consider how you were able to do this.
What kinds of knowledge about reading did you use? First, it is obvious that a lot more
than phonics knowledge was involved. Certainly your knowledge of phonics was helpful, but phonics alone would not have enabled you to interpret the texts. After all, in
the first paragraph, almost all of the vowels were omitted; in the second paragraph, all
of the letters of each word were included, but they were scrambled; and in the third
paragraph, only the beginning of each word was included. Yet none of these things pre-
vented you from reading the texts—you were able to use other kinds of information to
read past the gaps in the phonic information. Your background knowledge of the

subject, and your knowledge of how English works, also played an important part in enabling you to predict the words you were reading.

In his early work on reading, Goodman (1967) refers to three kinds of knowledge on which readers draw to gain meaning from text: semantic knowledge (knowledge of the world); syntactic knowledge (knowledge of the structure of the language; and graphophonic knowledge (knowledge of sound-letter relationships). The next three examples illustrate each kind of knowledge:

*The sun rises in the East and sets in the*_____.
(Your knowledge of the world predicts that the missing word is *West*.)

This animal is a klinger. This is another klinger. There are two _____.
(Your knowledge of how English works allows you to predict *klingers*, using other plural words as an analogy. The word is a made-up one, so background knowledge doesn't help here!)

*The flag is red, black, and y*_____.
(Here graphophonic knowledge is important. The letter *y* allows you to predict *yellow*. Without this cue you would have guessed that the missing word was a color, but not which one.)

In reality, however, readers use all three kinds of knowledge simultaneously. Indeed, effective readers draw on different kinds of knowledge depending on what they are reading and how much they know about the topic. For example, if the last sentence had read, "*The Aboriginal flag is red, black, and* ____," most Australian readers would have been able to predict the final word without any further cue. But readers from other countries, who may lack this knowledge, would need more cues from the text itself. If you reflect on your own reading, you'll be aware that you're able to read familiar material (e.g., an article on a topic about teaching) much faster than unfamiliar material (e.g., an academic paper on a topic you know nothing about).

When you are unable to bring personal knowledge and understanding of a topic to a text, you are effectively robbed of the ability to make use of a key resource for reading: what you already know. This has considerable implications for second language learners, who may not have the same cultural or world knowledge as the writer of the text. We will return to this later. For now, consider also the role that knowledge about the language system plays. If you are able to read another language yourself, but are not very fluent in the language, you will find that your reading relies much more on graphophonic cues than does your reading in English, and so you read much more slowly—the resources that are available to a fluent speaker of the language are not available to you. Many ESL children are also in this position when they read in English. Again, we will return to this point later.

Another major contribution to our knowledge of reading comes from schema theory. Originally the term was used to explain how the knowledge we have about the world is organized into interrelated patterns based on our previous experiences and knowledge. For example, if you go into a restaurant, you have certain expectations about what it will be like. Someone will bring you a menu, ask if you want a drink, and give you a check at the end. You will have a good idea how much of a tip you are expected to leave, and you will know how to use a credit card to pay for the meal. If you go to McDonald's, on the other hand, you will order from the counter, pay before you get the food, and not leave a tip. Knowing what to expect and how to behave in these two contexts comes from your previous experiences and from being part of a particular culture and society. The amount of tip to leave, and when to tip, are examples of this kind of cultural knowledge, which varies enormously from country to country—as anyone familiar with both North America and Australia is aware! Schema theory, applied to reading, proposes that effective readers likewise draw on particular kinds of culturally acquired knowledge to guide and influence the comprehension process (see Anderson and Pearson 1984). In one well-known study, two groups of adults, white North Americans and Native Americans, were asked to read and recall two letters describing a typical wedding of each group. There were clear cross-cultural differences in the way in which the same information was interpreted and recalled by the two groups (Steffenson, Joag-Dev, and Anderson 1979).

Wallace (1992) suggests that this schematic or in-the-head knowledge may be of two types: knowledge of the "content" or topic, and knowledge of the kind of genre. Think, for example, of what you are able to predict from these headings alone:

Bank Robbers Hold Hostages
Area Manager required, permanent position
The Sly Cat and the Clever Mouse

It is easy to predict that the first is a newspaper headline for a news report, the second a job advertisement, and the third a children's story. You will probably be able to predict a good deal of the content too. The first is likely to include details of a bank robbery, where and when it occurred, who the hostages are and how many there are, and so on. The job advertisement will probably include details of the position, the company it is with, criteria for the post, salary range, a reference number, and an email or postal address for applications. The story will probably begin with an orientation telling where the story is set and about the relationship of the characters, and in the course of the narrative the bad cat will end up being fooled by the intelligent mouse!

We know all this even before we begin to read. This information is in our heads, as a result of our familiarity with reading similar genres and reading about similar topics in the past; ultimately it comes from being participants in the culture in which these texts exist. In one sense, reading simply confirms what we know: we map our already existing experiences onto what we read. But what happens if our previous experiences have not provided us with this particular schematic knowledge, or if they have provided us with different schematic knowledge? Without the predictions you were able to make with these three texts, imagine how much more difficult they would be to comprehend. If you have ever read a newspaper from another English-speaking country, you will realize how much is taken for granted: the writer expects that you will know key people, key events, and key issues relevant to that country. Without this assumed knowledge, many newspaper stories are not easy to make sense of. And there will always be topics that we know little about and that are therefore very difficult to read about.

Even though we have the relevant knowledge, we still need to be "clued in" to what we are reading, and if we miss a clue, even our existing knowledge doesn't help us. The following text lacks a title. How much are you able to understand?

> The procedure is actually quite simple. First you arrange things into different groups. Of course, one pile may be sufficient, depending on how much you have to do. If you have to go somewhere else due to lack of facilities, then that is the next step; otherwise you are pretty well set. It is important not to overdo things. That is, it is better to do too few things at once than too many. In the short run this may not seem important, but complications can easily arise. A mistake can be expensive as well. . . . After the procedure is completed, one arranges the materials into different groups again. Then they can be put into their appropriate places. Eventually they can be used once more, and the whole cycle will then have to be repeated. (Adapted from Bransford and Johnson 1972)

Although you are able to read all the words, and at one level can "understand" individual sentences, you would probably find it very difficult to summarize the main points of this text. How do you know what the main points are when you don't have a sense of the overall meaning? (This places you in a similar position as ESL learners who are asked to summarize texts that contain content that is unfamiliar to them.) However, if you are told that the passage is about doing the laundry, the meaning suddenly becomes clear, and individual sentences are easily interpretable. You now have some in-the-head knowledge onto which to map the text. Yet what has changed? Certainly not the words on the page. What has changed is the nature of your interaction with the text—you are now reading about things that make sense to you and that link with your own experiences. What is clear from this example is that meaning does not reside solely in the words and structures of the text, but is constructed in the course of a transaction between the text and the reader.

Theories of Literacy Pedagogy

As a result of a range of views about what reading is, there are many theories of literacy pedagogy. At different times (and for reasons that are frequently political rather than educational), approaches such as phonics, whole-word, whole language, and critical are put forward as *the* method that will lead to successful literacy performance. Alan Luke and Peter Freebody (1990) argue, however, that the issue is not to do with which method is the most appropriate; rather, each of these general approaches emphasizes particular aspects of literacy. It is not that one program affords literacy and another doesn't, but rather that different programs emphasize different "literacies." Luke and Freebody suggest that there are four components of literacy success, and that successful readers need the resources to take on four related roles as they read: the roles *of code breaker, text participant, text user,* and *text analyst.* These are briefly discussed in the next section.

Reader as Code Breaker

As a *code breaker*, a reader needs to be able to engage in the "technology" of written script—that is, with the sound-symbol relationships, left-to-right directionality, and alphabet knowledge (this is the sort of knowledge that is central to the "back to basics" movements in North America, the United Kingdom, and Australia). It is true that alphabetic awareness is well-established as a significant factor in learning to read (see Ehri 1990), and children's development and ultimate success in reading may be hindered by misunderstandings or lack of knowledge about how to crack the code. A good literacy program will not ignore these elements. But as the other three roles suggest, code breaking, though necessary, is not sufficient for the successful reading of authentic texts in real social contexts—and the importance of knowing the code does not justify its teaching in contexts devoid of any real meaning.

Reader as a Text Participant

As a *text participant*, the reader connects the text with his or her own background knowledge—including knowledge of the world, cultural knowledge, and knowledge of the generic structure—in the sorts of ways discussed earlier in this chapter. Luke and Freebody cite an example of the ways in which cultural knowledge is related to reading comprehension, drawing on the work of Reynolds, Taylor, Steffensen, Shirey, and Anderson. In this example, a mix of eighth-grade Afro-American and Anglo-American students read a passage about "sounding," a form of verbal ritual insult predominantly found among black teenagers. While the Afro-American students correctly interpreted the text as being about verbal play, the Anglo-American students in general interpreted it as being about a physical fight. Despite the fact that their decoding skills were as good and possibly better than the Afro-American students, the Anglo-American students were unable to "read" the text in a way that matched the writer's intentions.

It is ironic, as Luke and Freebody point out, that in many standardized reading tests, the Afro-American students, in general, would probably have scored lower than their middle-class Anglo-American peers. Yet in this example, which acknowledges the role of cultural knowledge, we see that the Afro-American students in fact were the far more effective readers. Being a text participant, then, means having the resources to match text with appropriate content and cultural knowledge.

Reader as Text User

As a *text user*, a reader is able to participate in the social activities in which written text plays a major part, and to recognize what counts as successful reading in a range of social contexts. The interactions that children have around literacy events construct their understandings about how they are expected to read particular texts. For example, parents may ask particular kinds of questions as they read a book aloud with young children; teachers may model through their talk how to approach a character study in a piece of literature; or teachers may demonstrate through their questions what knowledge counts as being significant in an information text. For an interesting and readable account of how different socio-cultural groups take meaning from texts in different ways, and how they model different reader roles, see *Ways with Words* (Brice-Heath 1983).

Reader as Text Analyst

As *text analysts*, readers read a text as a crafted object, one that is written by an author who has a particular ideology or set of assumptions. An effective reader reads critically, recognizing in the text what is assumed, not said, implied, or unquestioned. Critical readers recognize that all texts, however authoritative they appear, represent a particular view of the world and that readers are positioned in a certain way when they read it. Clear examples of this reader-positioning technique are media advertisements that deliberately seek to manipulate the reader. Critical reading entails recognizing the many other ways in which texts of all sorts are written out of a particular belief system or ideology and how, though in more subtle ways than advertisements, and often less intentionally, these texts may also be manipulative. (See, for example, Cummins and Sayers 1995.)

Each of these roles foregrounds a particular aspect of reading. Because they are all integral to effective reading, a well-balanced literacy program will plan to make provision for the coherent development of each of them. But they should not be seen as representing a developmental "sequence," for each role can be developed at every level of reading. Indeed, as we have seen, there are good reasons for not simply focusing on code breaking with early readers, and, as we'll explore later, even very young readers can be shown how to read text critically.

Implications for ESL Learners

Many ESL students are effective readers who enjoy reading, and many are able to read in more than one language. As Jim Cummins (1996) has argued, being able to read in one's first language is one of the most important factors in learning to read in a second. But some children, particularly those whose first experience of learning to read is in their second language, may need particular kinds of support in learning literacy. We should also remember that most children's books are written with the assumption that their readers will be familiar with the cultural aspects of the story and will be already fluent in the spoken language.

The earlier discussion made it clear that the knowledge readers bring to the text is critical in their ability to get meaning from it. Of course, once we become fluent readers, we read to gain new information, although, as we have seen, even in this case there must still be some match between what the reader already knows and the information in the text. But when children are *learning* to read, it is important that they develop these new and challenging skills in the context of familiar or comprehensible content. Most teachers would accept that a very basic principle of good teaching is to go from what students already know to what they don't yet know, to move from the given (already known) to the new (what is yet to be learned), and this is very much the case with the teaching of early reading.

However, this does not imply that teachers should avoid any books that contain unfamiliar content or cultural aspects. On the contrary, part of learning a language involves learning about the culture in which it is used, and if we restrict what children read to the blandness of the basal reader, we do them a disservice by presenting a reductionist and limiting curriculum. So, rather than avoiding books that carry any unfamiliar cultural material (an almost impossible task anyway), the challenge for the teacher is to *build up* the knowledge and understandings that are relevant to the text the children will read, so that by the time the reader interacts with the text, the text will not be so unfamiliar. One major implication of the earlier discussion is that what the teacher does *before* a book is read is an extremely important part of the overall plan for using it with the class. Later in this chapter we look at a range of before-reading activities.

The earlier discussion also pointed to the role that familiarity with the language itself has in learning to read. Being unfamiliar with the language makes it almost impossible to predict what will come next. Here is an example of how this may affect reading. In one classroom, a student was asked to complete this sentence: *Although the light was red, the car . . .* We would expect the sentence to end something like *. . . the car continued,* or *. . . the car kept going.* Instead, the child completed the sentence to read *the car stopped.* He had not understood the word *although.* If he met this word in his reading, he would equally have been unable to predict the kind of meaning that followed it—that is, that the car did something unexpected in that context. The cues for predicting meaning that come from knowing the language would in this context have been unavailable to him. So, giving children opportunity to gain some familiarity with the language of the book before they come to read it is also important. Again, a later part of the chapter suggests some of the ways you might do this.

Without knowledge of the topic and with limited linguistic resources, a young reader has no choice *but* to rely on graphophonic knowledge. As we said earlier, being able to use this knowledge is an important part of reading, but relying on it too heavily means that children are limited in their use of other kinds of resources and in other reader roles they will be expected to play. Children who read slowly—painfully sounding out each letter, focusing on word by word—are often unable to carry meaning at the sentence level or across stretches of discourse, so they often lose the overall meaning of what they are reading. Ironically, however, poor readers have often been fed a diet of remedial phonics instruction, and while this may be appropriate for a few children, it is likely that for many young second language learners, this is precisely the area in which they don't need help. (Remember too that sounds and letters are very abstract concepts, particularly when the sounds don't match those children are accustomed to hearing in their mother tongue.) Rather, ESL learners need access to a linguistically and culturally rich reading environment, a range of reading strategies to bring to the process of reading, and a literacy program that aims to develop all the roles that effective readers take on.

Planning for Reading: Activities for Before, During, and After Reading

Reading activities should fulfill two major functions.

1. They should help readers understand the particular text they are reading.
2. They should help readers develop good reading strategies for reading other texts.

In other words, it's important that the instructional activities you use for helping learners comprehend a particular text also model the way effective readers read. For example, explaining all the unknown words before children read may help learners understand the text (or it may not if the learning load is too great), but it does not help them know what to do the next time they come to an unknown word. On the other hand, giving children strategies about what to do when they meet an unknown word not only helps them in that instance, but it also makes explicit strategies that can be transferred to other reading contexts.

A useful way to think about using a text with your class is to divide the planning into three sections: (1) what you will do before the reading; (2) what you and the children will do while the reading is going on: (3) and what you will do after the book has been read (see Wallace 1992). This overall plan is a useful framework that works whether you intend to read the book aloud yourself or whether you are planning for children to read by themselves or in small groups. The activities that follow are examples of what you might choose to do at each of these times. (You should select from these what is most useful and relevant for your students.)

To begin, try to predict what will be unfamiliar content or language for your students. Look for aspects of everyday life that may not be familiar to recently arrived children. Christmas, a visit to the beach, a visit to the zoo, a barbecue or picnic, an overnight stay with friends, birthday parties, school graduation, camps and excursions, surfing, watching a football match or baseball game, going to a disco, keeping pets, and many other aspects of life reflected in children's books are not taken for granted by all cultural groups. And there are considerable differences between families within any particular ethnic or cultural group, too. (Not all of these things will be part of your everyday life either, since they contain North American, British, and Australian examples!) Also note aspects of the language that may cause difficulty for students. These may include unfamiliarity with the genre; unknown connectives and conjunctions; use of pronouns, auxiliary verbs, or tenses; long sentences; or unfamiliar vocabulary, phrases, and idioms.

Before-Reading Activities

The purpose of these activities is to prepare for linguistic, cultural, and conceptual difficulties and to activate prior knowledge. They should aim to develop knowledge in relation to the *overall* meaning of the text, not to deal with every potential difficulty. As schema theory suggests, if students come to the text with a sense of what they will be reading about, reading becomes a much easier task because they have more resources to draw on. The reader will be less dependent on the words on the page and will be able to minimize the disadvantage of having less than native-speaker proficiency in the language.

There is another advantage of well-designed before-reading activities. Because learners will have some sense of overall meaning, they are likely to be able to comprehend more linguistically challenging language than they might otherwise be able to comprehend. It has been found, for example, that ESL children who heard a story initially in their mother tongue better understood unfamiliar language structures of the story when it was later read in English. The text can therefore also serve the purpose of extending learners' linguistic abilities by providing models of new language.

Here are some examples of **before-reading activities**. They all provide a context in which the teacher can guide learners into understanding the major concepts and ideas in the text. In discussion, try to use any particular vocabulary and language patterns that occur in the text; you can do this informally simply by using them as you interact with children.

✳ Predicting from Words

Put a word or phrase from the text on the board and ask children to say what they think it will be about, or what words they associate with the topic. Develop a **semantic web** based on the children's suggestions. Add a few words yourself that you know occur in the text, and discuss the meaning.

✳ Predicting from Title or First Sentence

Write up the title of the book, or the first sentence of the text, and get children to predict what kind of text it is (e.g., a narrative or an information text) and what the text will be about. You might wish to guide the class in a way that will best help them deal with the major concepts or events in the text to be read.

✳ *Predicting from a Key Illustration*

Photocopy a key illustration from the book and give children time in pairs or groups to say what they think the topic is about, or what the story will be. For example, based on a text about earthquakes the class would later be reading, one teacher gave the class a picture of the devastation after an earthquake and asked them to guess what had happened. She then introduced some new vocabulary that would occur in the text: *tremor, Richter Scale, shocks, aftershocks.* Almost all children were quickly able to relate these to the words they knew in their first language.

✳ *Sequencing Illustrations*

Give groups of children a set of pictures relating to the story, and ask the students to put them into a possible sequence.

✳ *Reader Questions*

Give children the title of the book or a key illustration and encourage them to pose questions they would like answered. The children using the earthquake text wrote questions such as *When did it happen? Where did it occur? How many people were killed? How big was it?* The teacher posted these questions on the wall, and the children looked for answers as they read the text later. (Here is another context for students to ask questions to which they want to find answers, as well as to practice question forms.)

✳ *Storytelling*

If you are using a narrative, tell the story simply, before reading it, using the illustrations from the book or doing simple line drawings of your own on the board as you are narrating it.

✳ *Storytelling in the Mother Tongue*

Tell the story in the children's first language (or invite a parent or other caregiver to do so) before reading it in English. If you have children who speak only English in the class, the experience will be valuable for them too. It will demonstrate your respect and acceptance of other languages, position the second language learners in the class as proficient language users, and show children that all languages are a means of communication.

✳ *Sharing Existing Knowledge*

For an information text, use an information grid such as that described in Chapter 4, and ask children to fill in what they already know about the topic. This is best done in groups.

The more time you spend on these kinds of activities, the easier the reading will be, and the more likely it will be that students read for meaning. Don't be tempted to reduce before-reading work to the explanation of a few key words! Of course, if the text you are using is part of a larger unit of work, much of this knowledge building will already be occurring in an ongoing way. One of the great advantages of an integrated approach is that reading occurs in a context where students are already developing an overall schema for the topic. And comprehension is much more likely to be improved when vocabulary and language are associated with broad concepts and recur in an ongoing context, than when instruction is in terms of single words or language items (see Carrell 1988).

During-Reading Activities

The purpose of these activities is to model good reading strategies. Good readers are actively involved in the text; they constantly interrogate and interact with it, and they predict what is coming. This is largely an unconscious process for fluent readers. The aim of during-reading activities is to make explicit some of these unconscious processes and to demonstrate the interactive nature of reading.

Once students have some idea of the genre and content of what they will be reading, it is time for the reading itself. Depending on the age and reading levels of the students, the first three activities described next are recommended as regular activities to use.

✳ Modelled Reading

It's useful to read the text aloud to the class the first time as a reading model for the students, using appropriate pausing and expression. Try to bring the text to life students need to see that print has meaning and is not simply a functionally empty exercise. With lower-level learners, remember that the more times something is read or heard, the more comprehension there will be. So don't read a text just once. A favorite book used in shared book time can be read again and again. As you read, encourage the children to see if their predictions were correct, but make clear that it doesn't matter if they weren't—often our predictions about things are wrong.

✳ Skimming and Scanning the Text

These are important reading strategies with which students need to become familiar. When readers skim a text, they read it quickly to get an idea of the general content. When they scan they also read fast, but the purpose is to look out for particular information. Searching down a telephone list, a train timetable, or a TV guide with the aim of finding a particular item are everyday examples of this. Some learners may have been trained to read in only one way—focusing on each word and every detail on the first reading. These students in particular will need practice in learning to skim and scan. It's important that you also make explicit the contexts in which we skim and scan, and point out that we read in different ways depending on our purposes for reading.

When students are going to read the text alone, and particularly if you haven't first read it aloud yourself, ask them first to skim it quickly. Explain that the purpose of this is to get a general idea of what it's about and a sense of the main ideas. Students can also scan the text to check any predictions they made. Again, it doesn't matter if these predictions were wrong; the actual process of having made predictions will encourage them to read the text more interactively. When students go into a text with a misconception, they are more likely to take note of the information presented there, because information that runs counter to one's expectations is usually more memorable than information that simply confirms what one already thinks. While the students are skimming the text on this first reading, they can also see if they can find the answers to any questions they asked.

✳ *Rereading for Detail*

Let the students read the text again, more carefully this time. The purpose of this is to make sure they have understood the information. Get them to underline or make a note of words or phrases they don't understand. They can discuss these in pairs. Remind them of strategies they can use to work out the meaning of unknown words, and point out that three things can help us: (1) the language that surrounds the word in the text; (2) our knowledge of the topic; and (3) what we know about similar words. Also remind them that knowing the exact meaning of every word is not essential every time we read, unless it prevents us from gaining the information we need.

Encourage students to use the following strategies when they are faced with an unknown word or phrase:

- Read to the end of the sentence to see if this helps in understanding the word.
- Look at the text that comes before and after the word; the word may be easier to understand later, with other clues to meaning.
- Use pictures to help guess the meaning.
- Think about the function of the word: is it a noun, verb, adjective?
- Look for the same word somewhere else; its meaning might be clearer there.
- Look for familiar word parts, such as prefixes and suffixes.
- Use a bilingual or English-English dictionary. Note that students should turn to a dictionary as a last resort and use it in combination with the other strategies. While dictionaries are a useful resource and students should be encouraged to use them when necessary, relying too heavily on a dictionary slows up reading and works against the development of the strategies listed above. It should also be remembered that definitions often don't adequately explain a meaning in the particular context in which it is being used, and that students may often select a wrong or inappropriate meaning.

You can place a similar sort of list on a wall. Remind students about these strategies whenever they read a new text. After they have finished reading, encourage discussion about how they dealt with the unknown words they came across.

❊ Shared Book

With young learners, shared book (sometimes called shared reading) can be a highly effective early reading activity. It involves using a Big Book in a group or whole-class activity. Shared book models how an experienced reader reads and how reading involves getting meaning from print. This understanding is particularly important when students are at an early stage of reading development.

For shared book, introduce the book through a range of before-reading activities, and then read it aloud several times, encouraging children to join in as they remember or recognize words or phrases. In later readings, using a pointer to point to words as you read helps children link the sounds of words with their shape on the page, and demonstrates left-to-right directionality and word spacing.

❊ Word Masking

Once a Big Book has been read several times, mask some of the words with small pieces of paper. Ask children to predict what the word is. Allow time to discuss alternative choices. For example, if the word is *replied* and someone guesses *said*, respond positively to this and use it as a basis for discussion. Among the words you mask, include not only "content" words, but also "functional" words, such as pronouns and conjunctions. As we mentioned earlier, these functional or grammatical words are important in enabling readers to use syntactic cues.

In later rereadings you can use this activity to develop vocabulary knowledge by focusing on alternatives for some of the words. Ask questions like *What's another word we could use here? What other words instead of said could the writer use?* This is a good way to develop vocabulary knowledge in context, and to build up word lists that can be displayed for children to use as a resource for their own writing.

❊ Pause and Predict

As you are reading, stop at significant points and ask questions like *What do you think is going to happen? What's she going to do? If you were (character's name), what would you do?* The goal here is to engage learners in the process of meaning making, not to have them verbalize the "right" answers.

❊ Shadow Reading

Record yourself reading the text, and use this recording with small groups of children or individuals, who should listen and follow the text from their own copy. Sometimes ask children to read aloud along with the tape. While reading aloud is not the same as "reading," shadowing is nevertheless a valuable activity because it demonstrates how meaning is made through text, and how intonation, stress, and the patterns of spoken language are related to the words on the page.

✳ *Summarizing the Text*

If students are unable to summarize what they have read, chances are strong that they have not understood the text fully, and that they are still unfamiliar with the content. (Remember how hard it was to summarize the "laundry text" when you didn't know what it was about.) Note that it isn't necessarily appropriate to summarize all kinds of texts. However, if this is something you want to focus on, here are some ways to help students practice summarizing skills.

- Get students to write a summary. Limit the maximum number of sentences or words they can use, pointing out that this means they must focus only on the most important points.
- Ask students to suggest a title for each paragraph.
- Either alone or with teacher support, have students write two or three sentences under each paragraph title and use these to write a short summary of the whole passage.
- If you are using a narrative, get students to retell it in shorter and shorter ways until it is as short as possible. Write this up on the board and then discuss with students the kind of information that is now missing.
- Have students explain the key points to someone else in less than one minute.
- Get groups of students to decide on one sentence from the text that best sums it up or is most central to the story. There will probably be some disagreement about this, but the discussion should help students sort out key points and help you see how they are interpreting the text.

✳ *Jigsaw Reading*

You need three or four different readings around the same topic. If you have varying reading levels in the class, include a simpler reading and a more challenging reading. Place students in expert/home grouping. Each group first becomes an "expert" in one of the readings and then shares the information in a mixed group. This kind of activity gives reading a real purpose, since the aim is to share what one has read with others. It is also a useful way of having readers at different levels work collaboratively (even the poorer readers will be able to contribute in the group since their reading will have information that other members in the group don't have). Finally, it provides an authentic context for developing summarizing skills, since each group of experts must decide on the key points they are later going to share with others. Depending on the level of the students, it may be useful to focus on note-making skills here, or to provide an information grid to guide students in locating key information.

✳ *Reading Aloud*

Listening to an experienced reader helps learners recognize that good readers make meaning, and it plays an important role in the development of reading competence. While this is especially important for young learners, the value of reading aloud should not be neglected with older learners. Serializing a longer book presents many opportunities for predicting what will happen. Or you may choose to simply whet children's appetites by reading only part of a book and leaving it for them to finish. It is also important to read nonfiction texts with students. This will help them get used to the more complex language patterns of transactional prose, and to familiarize them with different kinds of texts.

After-Reading Activities

These activities are based on the assumption that students are already familiar with the text, and no longer have basic comprehension difficulties in reading it. The activities use the text as a springboard, and may fulfill any of these three major purposes:

1. To use the now-familiar text as a basis for specific language study, such as to focus on a particular item of grammar, idiom, or phonic knowledge that occurs in the text.
2. To allow students an opportunity to respond creatively to what they have read, such as through art or drama activities.
3. To focus students more deeply on the information in the text, such as by using information transfer activities that represent the information in a different form (e.g., a time line or a diagram).

Well-designed after-reading activities usually require students to keep returning to the text and rereading it to check on specific information or language use.

✳ *Story Innovation*

Story innovation can be a teacher-led or small-group activity. Using the original story as a basis, key words are changed to make a new story, while retaining the underlying structure. For example, students could change the characters in the folktale *The Elephant and the Mouse* to a whale and a little fish. While the central meaning of the tale should remain the same (the weak helps the strong and they become friends), key words and events are changed to fit in with the new characters. As the changes are made, the story is written up on a large sheet of paper.

✳ *Innovating on the Ending*

Write a new ending to a story, in groups or as a whole class.

* **Cartoon Strip**

In groups, or individually, students turn the story into a cartoon strip, using the words of the dialogue in the original to write in the "speech bubbles."

* **Readers' Theatre**

In its simplest form, you provide a group of children with copies of the story. Each chooses the dialogue of one of the characters to read, while other children share the narration. This can be practiced until it is word perfect and then performed to the class. Readers' Theatre is a much better context for children reading aloud than the traditional "reading around the class," since it allows them a chance to *practice* the reading (which is what adults would do if they knew they were going to read in front of others), and it provides a meaningful purpose for the reading.

Depending on their reading and language levels, some children can write scripts based on the story. Puppets can also be used in Readers' Theatre.

* **Wanted Posters**

Ask students to design a wanted poster for a character in a story, incorporating as much of the information in the text as possible (who they are, their description, what events are associated with them, and so on).

* **Story Map**

A story map is a visual representation of the main features of a story. It can be drawn after a story is read, or it can involve an ongoing process of adding details as the story is progressing.

* **Time Lines**

Texts that incorporate the passage of time lend themselves to a time line. These include narratives and some information texts (e.g., those that relate to events in history, or to the description of life cycles or processes). Children can also illustrate key events on the time line.

* **Hot Seat**

This activity is based on a narrative text. Children are seated in a circle, with one chair being designated the "hot seat." The student in the hot seat represents a character from a book that has been shared by the class. Other students ask him or her questions to find out more about the character's life. Questions might include the following: *Where do you live? Can you tell us about some of your friends? What do you most enjoy doing? How did you feel when . . . ? What do you think of (another character in the book)?* Children take turns being in the hot seat. While they are free—and should be encouraged—to invent information, they mustn't say anything that is inconsistent with the story or with what has been learned from the other hot-seaters.

After a while, play around with the time frame of the story by moving into the past or the future. Get children to stand and slowly walk counterclockwise in a circle, and as they are walking tell them they are time travelers going backward in time. Give the children a specific point in time, such as "Now it's seventy years ago and the old woman in the story is just a little girl." Continue the hot seat activity as before, constructing an earlier life for one of the characters. Later, children can move clockwise around the circle, forward in time, until young characters in the story are now old people, or perhaps they are now dead and are being remembered by others.

In this way the original story takes on a further life, and children will have a wealth of ideas for their own story writing. Rereading the original story, now that so much is "known" about the entire lives of some of the characters, also becomes a very thought-provoking and enriching reading experience.

✳ Freeze Frames

Freeze frames are a kind of drama activity that show a series of tableaux representing key stages in a story. Each tableau is a "still," with the students taking the role of specific characters. Simple props can be used. The audience members close their eyes while the group prepares the first tableau, and at a signal from the group, they open their eyes and look at it for about ten seconds. Then they close their eyes again while the group prepares the second tableau, and so on until the story is told. The audience thus views the actions as a series of frozen frames. Groups will need some time to prepare this. They first need to decide on what the key stages are (see the previous chapter for the overall structure of a narrative), then decide how they will represent them, and finally practice moving from one to the other as quickly as possible (otherwise the audience will not keep their eyes closed!). Since freeze frames do not require students to say anything at the presentation stage, even newly arrived children will be able to participate fully in the freeze frame. At the same time, the preparation of the frames requires students to discuss important elements of the story and make decisions about how to portray the characters and events.

✳ Cloze

Traditional cloze exercises, the device of deleting words from a text, can be based on the text that has been read. When you make the deletions, you should keep at least the first and last sentences intact so that students have a context in which to read the text. Encourage students first to read the cloze straight through before they attempt to fill in the gaps. To provide extra support for lower-level readers, you can give students a list of the words that have been left out.

Originally, cloze exercises were aimed at testing rather than teaching. However, in more recent years, their potential for developing learners' reading strategies has been recognized. A well-constructed cloze can give you information about what kinds of strategies children are using to predict meaning, and it can help children think about their own reading strategies. Traditional cloze involves deleting every fifth, sixth, or seventh word, and it encourages readers to reference backward and forward in the text to work out what the missing words are likely to be. It therefore mirrors the kind of reading strategies used by proficient readers. However, cloze exercises can also be used more selectively, with only certain kinds of words deleted. For example, you can choose to delete key content vocabulary that is integral to the topic, or grammatical items such as adjectives, connectives, pronouns, past tenses, and so forth. Cloze exercises are often more successful when students work in pairs, since there will be discussion about why certain choices are made. The aim is not simply for children to get the "right" answer but to become aware of what they do when they read.

After finishing a cloze, always allow time for discussion. Children should be able to *justify* the words they have chosen and *explain* to others their rationale for their choice. To make this discussion easier for the class, put the cloze on an overhead so that it is easier to talk about the possible and most appropriate choices with the class. (Remember that while there is often a range of possible and appropriate words to fill "content" gaps, there is a much smaller range of options for grammatical items.)

✳ Monster Cloze

This consists of only a title and gaps. It can be based on the text the students have read, or on a summary of it. Write the *title* of the passage on the board in full. The passage itself, however, consists of only the gaps! Students guess the missing words (in any order), and the teacher writes in any correct words in the appropriate gap. After the sentences are partially completed, students should be able to predict more and more of the words of the passage by using their knowledge of the topic and of the language.

✳ Vanishing Cloze

This is a further variation on cloze. Select a short excerpt from the text the students have read (three or four sentences only, or a shorter section for beginners) or a summary of it. Write the excerpt on the board, and ask students to read it aloud together. Erase one word from anywhere in the text. Students read it again, putting back the missing word. Erase another word and repeat the process. Continue until all the words are removed, so that students are now "reading" from memory. It's important that after each word is removed, students repeat the reading; this requires them to replace more and more words each time. These repeated readings are especially helpful if the text contains a tricky grammatical structure or subject-specific vocabulary that the students are currently learning, since it provides a context for repetition that is both fun and challenging.

✳ *Text Reconstruction*

Cut an excerpt from the text into paragraphs or sentences. Students must put the sentences or paragraphs in the right order and explain why they have chosen that order. This is a good context for focusing on text cohesion and drawing attention to reference words and conjunctions.

✳ *Consonant Groups*

Children sort a number of small objects (e.g., a pencil, pen, paper, box, ball, lid, leaf) or pictures of objects into groups, depending on their initial sound. You can use this either as a general reading activity, or you could base the words on those in the text the children have just read. For young children, you could make up class collections of pictures that are kept in boxes labeled with their initial letter. Encourage children to bring pictures from magazines to add to the collection. These "consonant boxes" can also be used for sorting activities.

✳ *Phonic Families*

Use a familiar Big Book and the masking technique to focus on how particular sounds are represented by particular letters or clusters of letters (e.g., the sound /ai/ as represented by *igh*). Begin to build up lists of words that contain the same sound and are spelled the same way.

✳ *Jumbled Sentences*

For beginner readers, take a sentence from the text and write it on a strip of cardboard. Cut up the sentence into words. Children must reconstruct the sentence by putting the words into the right order. For very early readers, make this a simpler task by providing the model sentence on a separate strip. Children then place the cut-up words on top of the matching words on the sentence strip.

✳ *Picture and Sentence Matching*

Take about six illustrations with matching sentences from the book. Cut them up into separate pictures and sentences. Children match the pictures with the appropriate sentences.

✳ *True/False Questions*

Children decide on whether a number of statements about the text are true or false. Make sure that these involve inferential as well as literal comprehension. Literal statements can be checked directly against the information in the text, whereas the truth of inferential statements needs to be inferred from the text. Here are examples of both types.

Sentence in the text: *The earthquake struck at three o'clock in the afternoon.*
Literal statement: *The earthquake struck at three o'clock. TRUE OR FALSE?*
Inferential statement: *The earthquake struck during the daytime. TRUE OR FALSE?*

In general, inferential statements (and questions) give you a better idea of how much readers have understood, since literal questions can often be answered correctly without comprehension of meaning (for an example of this, see Gibbons 1993, 70).

✳ Questioning the Text

As we discussed earlier, being able to read critically is an important part of being truly literate. To alert children to the hidden messages of text, and the underlying assumptions about reality made by the writer, teachers need to ask different kinds of questions and use different kinds of activities from those normally associated with text comprehension. Here are some examples.

- Focus on the pictures and on what the characters are doing. For a book where family life is depicted, you might ask things like *What is the mother doing? What is the father doing? Do all mothers and fathers do these things? What other things do mothers and fathers do?* Seek to show children that books do not necessarily depict the "whole truth," and that other kinds of reality and role options also exist. Try to be inclusive of all children's experiences.
- Discuss with children what the characters are like. Ask: *What words are used to describe the characters? When the characters are mentioned in the text, what words can you find in the text that tell you about them?* This will focus children's attention on what the characters are doing, and how they are described. It will also require them to go back to the text to reread parts of it with a more critical perspective.
- Make lists with the children of words or ideas that are associated with key people in the text. This is an interesting activity to use with information texts, too. In one classroom, the children were comparing how a particular sports writer wrote about top male and female athletes, and what kinds of information and descriptive words were included (or omitted). They found that considerably more was written about the physical appearance of the women, including words relating to their attractiveness, than was written about the men. It was also noted that some were mothers! Conversely, much more relevant information (about their athletic prowess and previous career) was included for the men, but much less space was devoted to information about their family life. Yet until the children set out to look for these associations, or collocations, and list the kinds of information the text included, they had not noticed these differences. When helping children develop critical perspectives on what they read, remember that it is also important to look at what is *not* said.

- Have children rewrite a folktale, changing the key physical or personality characteristics of the characters.
- Talk with the children about stereotyping. In one classroom, the children were reading a story set in Fiji, which contained very stereotypical views of life on a tropical island. As one of the children in the class had recently arrived from Fiji, the teacher assigned him the role of informant, whom other children could question about everyday life in Fiji. Later, having decided that the book did not represent the Fiji they had learned about from their classmate, a group rewrote the book. They had learned a useful lesson: what you read is not necessarily "true."

A word of warning when you are helping children read critically. Taking a critical perspective may lead into discussions that are highly connected to children's lives. Be prepared for this, and treat the personal stories that may result with empathy and sensitivity. Avoid forcing children to contribute to any discussion they are not comfortable with; however, in an open and nonthreatening environment, we should try not to shy away from the issues that the books themselves present. And equally important, children should not be left feeling helpless or positioned as "victims." Positive strategies and ways of action should result from critical discussions, such as the rewriting of the book about Fiji. Other actions might include making new and more inclusive illustrations for a text, or a class letter to a newspaper editor.

Choosing Books: A Reason for Turning the Page

There is considerable evidence to suggest that, while overall language development supports reading, so too does reading support language development (Wallace 1988, 1992). Language is learned through reading; it is not simply a prerequisite for it. Given appropriate texts, learners develop their language skills in the course of reading itself, perhaps because the patterns of language are "open to notice" in written language in a way that they are not in spoken language. So the more fluently and widely that ESL students read, the more exposure to the second language they will gain.

Research also suggests that second language learners are able to determine the meanings of quite large numbers of unfamiliar English structures *if* they are presented in the context of meaningful sentences (see, for example, Elley 1984; Wallace 1988). This implies that particular language structures don't have to be in the active repertoire of learners (i.e., able to be used) to be understood in reading. As long as learners have a sense of the overall meaning of what they read, wide reading is an effective way of learning *new* language items, not simply of reinforcing or practicing old ones.

One clear implication of this view of the role of reading in language development is that the books that children read must provide a rich linguistic environment. In the past, many books used in school were written simply to "teach reading." Here is an example of the kind of language common to such books:

Page 1 See John. See Susan.
Page 2 See John and Susan run.
Page 3 Here is Rex.
Page 4 Here is the ball. See Rex run.
Page 5 Run Rex run. Run Susan run! Run John run.

It is true that a few children appear to gain some satisfaction from being able to decode such books, but we should ask ourselves what they are learning about reading if this represents their major reading diet, and whether this route to reading is the most productive for second language learners.

First, books like this are in some ways much more difficult to read than a complete story, especially for young readers, because it is almost impossible to predict what will come next. Thus learners are forced into total reliance on phonics. Because they are led to concentrate on the visual and phonic characteristics of words, they are led away from an understanding of text as coherent language. Of course, the major rationale for the choice of words in this instance is not to present authentic language, but to present a particular sound or word as frequently as possible. But as Wallace (1988) comments, "Books that set out to teach reading are frequently not so much books as strings of sentences that do not connect to build up any kind of text with a beginning, a middle and an end" (150). The pages quoted here can in fact be read backwards, putting the last sentence first, without any loss or much change of meaning! Learners are thus encouraged to think that reading is a random activity that can apparently start or stop at any point in the text, and that we read words or sentences but not continuous text. Such books also seem to assume, quite wrongly, that short words are "easier" to read. Yet we have all had experience of very young children recognizing salient words in their environment, such as the McDonald's sign or their own name. And we have also probably had children who can happily read words like *dinosaur* or *Pokemon* but balk at words like *was*, *ball*, or *toy* in basal readers.

Texts like the one shown here are also functionally empty; there is little meaning to be had and no access to the rich models of language that are so important for ESL children. And finally, as many children, their teachers, and their families know, books like this are mind-numbingly boring.

We don't, of course, want learners to learn lessons like this. Rather, as Wallace (1988) succinctly puts it, "We want to give learner-readers a reason for turning the page" (151). Good readers read for pleasure, to extend their worldview, to read more about what interests them, or to find out things they want or need to know about. And these are the sorts of purposes for reading we want children to have. As I argued earlier,

Books like this are
mind-numbingly boring

children should not be restricted to the familiar, the known, and the "easy," and fed a watered-down version of written language. Rather, as the activities in this chapter aim to do, the challenge for teachers is to find ways of giving learners *access to* well-written children's literature and relevant information texts.

There are many criteria for choosing books, and it is beyond the scope of this chapter to discuss these in detail. But for beginning readers who are learning to read in their second language, books that have the following characteristics will be supportive of early reading.

- Repetitive language that becomes familiar to children so that they can begin to join in (e.g., *Run, run, as fast as you can, you can't catch me, I'm the gingerbread man*).
- A repetitive event that builds up into a cumulative story (e.g., *First the farmer, then his wife, then the child, then the dog, then the cat, then the mouse . . . all tried to pull up the giant turnip*). Many stories include a repetitive structure of this sort, which decreases the comprehension load on ESL children. Once they understand the event, they are able to transfer their understanding to each repetition.
- Universal themes (e.g., good triumphs over evil), universal motifs (e.g., three sons or daughters, the two eldest of whom are bad, the youngest of whom is good), and the teaching of moral behavior (e.g., kindness gets rewarded).
- Illustrations that clearly represent the meanings in the text and that can be used as cues to meaning.
- Clear print and well-laid-out pages that are not too "busy."
- Good, authentic models of language that doesn't sound contrived.
- Content and language that, while it might not be immediately accessible, can be "bridged" for ESL readers.
- Content and language that can be used to extend children's knowledge about reading and about the world.
- Content that is of interest and that will be enjoyable to read.

As this list suggests, probably one of the best ways to introduce reading to ESL children is by using fairytales. These seem to incorporate some kind of "universal schema" that children from all cultures are able to relate to. Because of their universality in terms of overall themes and motifs, they are likely to make sense to children in ways that other texts may not, and even where specific characters and settings in the stories are different, many cultures share basic stories in common.

For older learners who are reading longer factual texts, the following is also important:

- Clear overall text organization. The better organized a text is, the easier it is to understand, and the more the reader is able to engage in higher-level processes such as summarizing and inferring.

- Clear signaling devices. The structure and content of a well-organized text is highlighted by such devices as titles, headings, clear topic sentences, and text cohesion.
- Appropriate conceptual density. New concepts should be spaced, and contain sufficient elaboration to make them understandable.
- Good instructional devices, such as a logically organized table of contents, glossary, index, graphic overviews, diagrams, and summaries.

In addition, the choice of books to use with your students will be affected by a number of other factors, such as their age, interests, and overall reading abilities. It will also be affected by your purpose in using the book. Will the book be used as instructional material aimed to extend a student's reading skills, and thus be a little ahead of the student's independent reading ability? Or is the book intended as part of a wide reading program, and thus something that children should be able to read fairly independently? In terms of the overall reading program, do children have access to a range of books, and a range of genre types? As this chapter has suggested, how comprehensible a book is will also be determined by the kinds of activities you use and the kinds of interactions the children will be engaged in around the text. However, whatever the books you choose, seek to ensure that they will give children "a reason for turning the page."

In Summary

In this chapter we have seen how unfamiliarity with aspects of a text (the knowledge it assumes, the genre, or the language itself) may cause difficulties for second language readers. While in some cases this may lead you to decide not to use a book, it may be more important for learning if, instead, you find ways to build bridges into the text, through the kinds of activities you choose to do before, during, and after reading. In this way, ESL learners can gain access to a wider range of books and richer reading experiences. We have also discussed the inadequacies of approaches that see basic decoding skills as reading, and we have looked at how readers must learn to take on a number of "reader roles." These roles can be developed *simultaneously* as children progress in their reading. Finally, we have looked at the importance of choosing books that encourage children to read—and to want to go on reading.

Suggestions for Further Reading

CARRELL, P. 1988. "Interactive Text Processing: Implications for ESL/Second Language Reading Classrooms." In *Interactive Approaches to Second Language Reading*, ed. P. Carrell, J. Devine, and D. Eskey. Cambridge, UK: Cambridge University Press.

GARIBALDI ALLEN, V. 1994. "Selecting Materials for the Reading Instruction of ESL Children." *In Kids Come in All Languages: Reading Instruction for ESL Students*, ed. K. Spangenberg-Urbschat and R. Pritchard. Newark, DE: International Reading Association.

WALLACE, C. 1992. "Reading and Social Meaning." Chapter 5 in *Reading*, ed. C. Wallace. Oxford, UK: Oxford University Press.

6

Listening
An Active and Thinking Process

Listening is primarily a thinking process—thinking about meaning.   Michael Rost, *Listening in Action*

Making Sense of What We Hear

The teaching of listening is often assumed to "happen" in the process of the teaching of speaking; indeed many teaching programs and syllabuses refer to "listening and speaking" as a single unit, and so the specific teaching of listening is often overlooked. Yet in terms of learning, and second language learning in particular, listening is a key to language development: understanding what is said in a particular situation helps to provide important models for language use. While most elementary classrooms are busy and exciting places for children, they are also frequently quite noisy. And even if this noise is kept to a minimum, there is usually a level of background buzz that may make it very difficult for children to comprehend what is said given that it is in a second language. (As you might have experienced yourself, background noise tends to interfere with comprehension far more if you are listening to a less familiar language.)

The process of listening is in many ways similar to the process of reading. Both involve comprehension rather than production, and both involve the active construction of meaning. To begin, try this listening test with a colleague.

One of you should read aloud one short paragraph from a book. The other should try to "shadow" the reader *only* by listening (not reading) and repeating as closely as possible the words *as they are being read*. You will probably find that the person who is "shadowing" will be only a syllable or so behind the reader. Now do the same thing again—but this time the reader should read the passage backwards. How easy is it now to "shadow"? If you are the person shadowing, you will probably have found it a much more difficult task, and you will probably find you are much further behind the reader. Why should this be, given that the individual words and the sounds are exactly the same?

The answer, of course, is that the second reading doesn't make sense: there is no meaning for the listener. What the listener is hearing in the second reading is simply a string of unconnected words. But to listen effectively we need to do more than simply recognize sounds and words. We need more than the acoustic information to gain meaning, just as in reading we need more than phonic information. Like reading, effective listening depends on the expectations and predictions about content, language, and genre that the listener brings to the text. And so, just like reading, listening is an active process that depends not only on decoding the acoustic information—the sounds—but also on the listener's in-the-head knowledge about the world and about the structure of the language. That is why shadowing the first reading was much easier than shadowing the second reading: you were able to draw on more sources of information.

To make the same point in another way, here is another listening activity. Imagine this time that you are *listening* to the story below. (Ideally, get someone to read it aloud.) At certain points you are asked to predict what happens next.

Once upon a time there was a very rich farmer who spent many evenings counting his gold. He thought of nothing else except his gold. He loved no one in the world and no one ever visited him. But one dark, cold and snowy night . . .
WHAT DO YOU THINK IS GOING TO HAPPEN?

. . . there was a knock on the door. The rich farmer opened the door, and there stood a poor, old, thin man.
WHAT DID THE OLD MAN SAY?

"Kind farmer," said the old man, "please give me shelter and a piece of bread."
WHAT DID THE FARMER SAY?

"Get away from my door," the farmer said angrily. "I have nothing to give you."

You were probably able to predict the answers to the questions easily—not the exact wording, but certainly the overall meaning. You can probably predict the overall story line as well. Yet you did not get all this information from what you heard alone.

In the last chapter, we noted how earlier models of reading saw it as being no more than decoding phonics. Earlier models of listening paralleled this. The process of listening was seen as one where the listener segmented a stream of speech into its constituent sounds, linked these to form words and then chained these words into clauses, sentences, and finally whole text. Nunan (1990) refers to this model of listening as "the listener as tape recorder," implying that the learner is a passive receiver of spoken language who takes no active part in making meaning. By contrast, more recent models of listening see the listener as what Nunan refers to as a "meaning builder." As in the process of reading, the listener is seen as taking an active role: listeners construct an interpretation of what they hear using not only the sounds of the language, but also, just as in reading, their available schema and knowledge of the language system.

When we think about the listening process, the notion of a "script" is useful. Just as in a play script, when the lines the actors speak are prewritten, in listening we draw on those "scripts" that are familiar to us through our previous experiences. Imagine, for example, that you meet a friend who has just returned from an overseas trip. When you ask her how the journey was, she comments:

> *It was good except for where I was sitting on the plane. They wouldn't let me move. The seat was . . .*

What sorts of things do you think your friend is going to talk about?

Who are the "actors" in this script?

What are the sources of the knowledge you need in order to interpret this, in order to predict what your friend is likely to say?

Anyone familiar with plane travel will have a good idea what is likely to be said. Perhaps the seat was too cramped, or perhaps she had requested an aisle or window seat but didn't get it. Maybe she was sitting next to someone unpleasant, or she was near a crying baby. *They* refers to the air stewards, or possibly the ground staff at check-in. The actors in this script are your friend and the steward (and possibly the ground staff) with whom she spoke about the problem, and possibly other passengers. The sources of knowledge that you used to interpret this snippet of conversation are your own experiences of air travel, or what you have learned from others' experiences.

On the other hand, if you had never experienced air travel, or heard about it from others, none of this interpretation and prediction would be possible. Again, note the similarity to the process of reading and the importance of background knowledge of the topic in understanding what we hear. Once more, it is clear that understanding what is said is not simply dependent on the sounds we hear.

Consequently, listening tasks in the classroom, just like reading tasks, are far more demanding if children have no previous knowledge on which to draw. Lack of comprehension is likely to be due to this, just as much as to the fact that learners may find certain sounds difficult to discriminate. Practice in sound discrimination in a listening program, just like the teaching of phonics in the reading program, is necessary but not sufficient to ensure comprehension. And for most children, difficulty in discrimination between particular pairs of sounds and their pronunciation does not remain a problem for long. Before considering some examples of listening activities and tasks, let's look briefly at the kinds of contexts in which listening occurs.

Types of Listening

Nunan (1990) has suggested that listening occurs in four types of contexts, which he sets out as a matrix (see Figure 6–1). First, it may be one-way, where the listener is not called upon to respond verbally (such as listening to the radio or to a lecture), or it may be two-way, where two or more people take on the roles of listener and speaker in turn (such as in a conversation). Listening can also broadly involve two types of topic: everyday interpersonal topics, the sort of everyday chat we all engage in with friends; and more information-based topics, the kind of talk that occurs in the classroom, or in contexts where the purpose is to gain information of some kind. Figure 6–1 shows how these four types of contexts produce a two-by-two matrix. Some examples of each of the four listening contexts are included.

Note that this is a very simplified picture of listening contexts; in reality the topics about which people speak cannot be classified so discretely, and it may sometimes be difficult to discriminate between what might be thought of as "chat" and "information getting." Nevertheless this matrix does represent the broad range of contexts for listening, and it is therefore useful as a programming device to check whether students are experiencing a *range of situations* in which to practice listening skills.

Generally, the easiest listening context for learners involves the sorts of situations found in Quadrant A, and to a lesser extent (because the topics may be less familiar)

two-way

QUADRANT A *Taking part in:* a conversation at a party a conversation at the bus stop about the weather a chatty phone call to a friend	**QUADRANT C** *Taking part in:* a job interview a conversation involving the giving of directions or instructions a phone inquiry about buying a computer
QUADRANT B *Listening to:* someone recounting a personal anecdote someone telling a story someone telling a joke	**QUADRANT D** *Listening to* the radio or TV news a lecture phone information (e.g., a recorded timetable, or instructions for paying a bill)

interpersonal topics ·· information-based topics

one-way

FIGURE 6–1.   *Contexts for Listening*

Quadrant C. Listening here is two-way, so listeners have a chance to ask for clarification or signal that they don't understand. And as Chapter 1 suggested, most ESL children quickly learn to talk to others and comprehend what is said to them in face-to-face contexts, when the talk is about everyday and familiar topics and where the visual context itself can be an aid to comprehension, such as some of the examples in Quadrant A.

However, not all situations that fall within this quadrant are easy for learners. Understanding what is said on the phone can be quite demanding for young learners. As the discussion about the mode continuum in Chapter 3 suggested, more linguistic resources are needed the further we move away from "here and now" language. And so a phone call, even though it is two-way and may be about familiar topics, may be a difficult task: while speakers must make everything explicit through language alone, listeners must also reconstruct the intended meaning from language alone. In addition, they must do it in "real time," without the time for reflection that is possible in reading.

One-way listening is generally more difficult than two-way because listeners don't have an opportunity to ask for clarification, or to slow down the text they are listening to. Quadrant D tasks are also likely to involve less familiar topics than those in Quadrants A and B, and probably represent the most demanding listening tasks for ESL students.

Implications for Teaching

As the previous section suggests, approaches to the teaching of listening should be primarily focused on meaning. To this end, here are a selection of listening activities that can be integrated within your regular program. They are divided into two groups, those that involve two-way listening and those that involve one-way listening. All the activities involve the learners taking some action, since we can never know what is going on in someone's head (in this case how well they are comprehending). In this way, it is only by seeing what a learner *does* as a result of listening that we can recognize whether effective listening has taken place.

Introducing How to Listen

Many children in today's world are unused to quiet, and have never learned to listen perceptively to specific sounds. In preparation to listening in the educational context, the following three activities, though not specifically language-based, help to sensitize children to the need to listen actively and perceptively.

✳ *What Can You Hear?*

Ask the children to be completely silent. Take some time to let them relax. They might want to close their eyes. When there is no sound within the classroom, ask them to listen to see what sounds they can hear: these will be mostly from outside the classroom. Give them several minutes to concentrate on this task, and then ask them what they heard. Possible answers might involve a dog barking outside, a truck going past, someone coughing, a baby crying, people talking, a chair squeaking, and so on. As a follow-up to this task for older students, you could also ask which of these sounds they would not have heard a hundred years ago.

✳ Sound Bingo

Make a selection of Bingo cards with the names of sounds on them, such as footsteps, someone laughing, a dog barking, a baby crying, the sound of rain, the sound of traffic, glass breaking, and so forth. Alternatively, draw pictures to illustrate the sounds. You will also need a "sound tape" of these sounds. As children hear a sound, they cover the word or picture on their card. The first person to have all the pictures covered is the winner.

✳ Sound Stories

Using a sound tape, play three different sounds to the children. In groups they make up a story in which all three sounds are significant.

Two-Way Listening

One of the most important things that ESL learners need to be able to do is ask for clarification when they don't understand something. So model and practice phrases like these:

> *Excuse me, I'd like to ask something.*
> *I'm sorry, I don't understand. Can you repeat that?*
> *I'm sorry, I didn't hear that. Can you say it again, please?*
> *Did you say . . . ?*
> *Sorry for interrupting, but would you mind repeating that?*

Remind students to use phrases like these *whenever* they don't understand something. It is a good idea to have them written up on a poster and displayed, so that their use becomes a classroom "norm," both when students are talking to each other and to you. You do not want your students to become so accustomed to "missing" bits of what is said that they begin to accept this as an inevitable part of their school experience! Some students not familiar with Western cultural norms may not be accustomed to these kinds of interruptions and may see them as extremely impolite, especially to a teacher. Reassure them that you want to be sure they understand what you say, and that a polite interruption or a request for clarification will help them do this.

Any interactive problem-solving task is a context for practicing interactive listening, for in these situations it is very likely that students will need to work out communication difficulties and clarify ideas. The spoken language activities discussed in Chapter 2 are therefore also listening activities. Some additional activities are described next. Remember to encourage the students to ask for clarification or repetition whenever they need to.

✳ *Describe and Draw*

This is a barrier game that can be done as a teacher-directed activity or between pairs of students, or with one student directing the class. One person draws a picture or series of shapes on a piece of paper. The other students can't see what is being drawn. At the same time, the artist gives instructions to a partner about what to do:

> *Draw a circle in the middle of the paper.*
> *Draw a big triangle on top so that it touches the circle.*
> *Under the circle, draw a . . .*
> *On the left, draw a . . .*

✳ *"If You Are . . ."*

This activity is adapted from Rost (1991). Like the previous activity, the students must follow directions, but this time the directions vary depending on the characteristics of individual students. It requires students to listen very carefully to the instructions. As in the previous tasks, encourage students to ask you to repeat or clarify information. Here is an example.

> *Write your name on the paper. If you are a boy, write it on the left. If you are a girl, write it on the right.*
> *Write your telephone number. If you are sitting beside a window, write it in red. If you are sitting anywhere else, write it in green.*
> *How do you come to school? If you take a bus to school, write the word* bus *inside a triangle. If you come by car, write the word* car *inside a square. If you walk, write the word* walk *inside a rectangle.*

You can make this quite a complex listening task for older or more able ESL students.

✳ *Map Game 1*

Give students identical maps, but with some road and building names removed. Map A should have the information that is not on Map B and vice versa. Collaboratively, but without showing each other their maps, the students must find out the missing names using questions like these:

> *What's the name of the road opposite the post office?*
> *What building is on the left of the post office?*

✳ Map Game 2

With identical and completed maps, students agree on a starting point. Student A then directs Student B to a destination unknown to Student B. When the instructions are complete, the student who has been following the instructions should end up in the right place! Here's an example:

Go along the street.
Turn left. You pass the post office on your left.
When you get to the traffic lights, turn right.
Just past the park there is a building.
Where are you?

Barrier games like this make ideal interactive listening activities since clarification questions are almost certain to occur as the listener seeks more information (*Did you say "left"? Can you repeat that? Is it near the station?*)

✳ Interviews

These can be based on members of the class, or students may carry our interviews in order to gain information about a class topic (see Chapter 4). In the process of the interview, the interviewer will need to focus closely on the interviewee's responses and perhaps ask further questions based upon the information that the interviewee is providing. This situation can provide an authentic and challenging listening task.

✳ Jigsaw Listening

This activity is based on an expert/home grouping and is similar to Jigsaw Reading described in Chapter 5. (Also see Chapter 2, and the Glossary, for a fuller description.) You will need to have a cassette player for each group. Like jigsaw reading, each group has a different set of information (in this case, to listen to) and in which they become "experts." Later they are regrouped, share their information with members of their new group, and listen to others' information. Different kinds of information sources can be used. For example, for a narrative, each group might have a part of the story. Or, if students are collecting factual information, each group might have a section of a report. One group may have information about the habitat of an animal, one about its feeding habits, another about what it looks like. Alternatively, each group could have information about a different animal, and the information could then be pooled. Or you could base the listening task on a procedural text (see Chapter 4), with each group having a few steps of the overall procedure. Remember, though, that a listening text needs to be processed in "real time," so the texts should not be too long, and they will probably need to be simpler than for reading. Depending on the difficulty of the text, you may prefer to let each group listen to the text more than once.

❋ *Split Dictation*

Make two gapped versions of a text, with each text having different gaps. In pairs students must complete the text by reading to each other the parts they have, and filling in the blanks for the parts they don't have, so that collaboratively they complete the whole text. Students can take it in turns to read sentence by sentence (see Figure 6–2). Children should not show each other their papers.

❋ *Dictogloss*

This is a listening activity that integrates listening with speaking, reading, and writing, and is described fully in the Glossary.

One-Way Listening

Many reading tasks can be adapted to use as listening tasks. In addition, as we have seen earlier in the chapter, listening, like reading, is facilitated when students have the

Partner A

1 Insects have caused much suffering _____ .
2 _____ have died of malaria.
3 This is a disease _____ .
4 Insects _____ .
5 _____ infects people with sleeping sickness.
6 _____ spreads bubonic plague .

Partner B

1_____ for human beings.
2 Millions of people _____ .
3 _____ which is spread by mosquitoes.
4 _____ spread many other diseases.
5 The tsetse fly _____ .
6 The rat flea _____ .

FIGURE 6–2. *Split Dictation*

relevant schematic or "in-the-head" knowledge. You may find it helpful at this point to go back to the before-reading activities listed in Chapter 5, since these activities are as important for listening as they are for reading, and they should form a part of the preparation for a specific listening task. This is especially the case in one-way listening, where learners will not have the opportunity to ask questions.

One-way listening usually involves either listening for a specific piece of information (e.g., listening to a recorded message for the time of a train), or listening with the aim of getting general information (e.g., listening to the news). Make sure that the tasks you use provide a balance between these two purposes.

LISTENING FOR SPECIFIC INFORMATION

✳ *Hands Up*

Give the students a set of questions based on a listening text. As they hear the piece of information that provides them with the answer, they raise their hands. They should have a chance to look at the questions before they hear the text.

✳ *Information Extraction Task 1: Listening for Facts*

Students listen to any documentary program or video that presents a number of facts and figures. Or they could listen to a recording of bus or train times. Prepare a sheet in chronological order corresponding to the facts as they are presented. Students must transfer the information as they listen. For example, if students are listening to information about a country, they listen specifically for particular pieces of information (see Figure 6–3). Where students already know something about the topic, encourage them to predict as many of the answers as they can *before* listening, so that they will be listening more actively and confirming or correcting their answers as they listen.

✳ *Information Extraction Task 2: Listening for Opinions*

Students listen to a recording of a debate (it could be one they took part in or one from another class). They make notes summarizing only one point of view. This is more challenging if the "debate" is not a formal one, but a discussion between several people

> - Name of a country
> - Where it is
> - Population
> - What language(s) people speak
> - Largest city
> - ?
> - ?

FIGURE 6–3. *Information Extraction*

who may share some points of view but not others. Students must then pay close attention to what is said in order to extract information appropriately and selectively.

LISTENING FOR GENERAL INFORMATION

❋ *Spot the Difference*

Record two versions of a story, or "invent" two news bulletins or two procedural texts that have minor changes of detail. Play one version to the students and ask them to listen for overall meaning. Play it a second time so that students become familiar with it. Give students a written version of the same text. Then play the alternative version. Students must "spot the difference" between the written version and the alternative oral version, and circle the words or phrases on the print version when they hear differences.

Version A

Just as Jack had taken all he could carry, the giant opened one eye and saw Jack. "Who are you?" he roared. He opened the other eye, and then he stood up. Jack could hardly see his head, it was so far away. He turned and ran and started to climb down the beanstalk as fast as he could. The giant strode after him, and Jack felt sure he was about to die!

Version B

Just as Jill had taken all she could carry, the giant opened one of his eyes and saw Jill. "Who are you?" he shouted. He opened the other eye, and then he stood up. Jill could hardly see his head, it was so far away. She turned and ran and began to climb down the beanstalk as fast as she could. The giant ran after her, and Jill felt sure she was about to be killed!

❋ *Picture Dictation*

Students have a number of jumbled pictures that tell a story or give a recount. Read a text that tells the story in its correct sequence. As you read the text, students put the pictures in order.

❋ *Matching Game (Listening)*

Students have several pictures, each labeled with a number. The teacher describes one of the pictures, giving each description a letter. Students then match the pictures with the description, saying which number goes with each letter. This is more challenging if the pictures are similar in most details.

❋ *Oral/Aural Cloze*

Give students a cloze exercise with random or focused deletions (see discussion of cloze exercises in Chapter 4 and the Glossary). Read the complete text to the students, who fill in the blanks.

The Sounds of English

Depending on the particular dialect spoken, English has around forty-four distinctive sounds or phonemes. Phonemes make a difference to the *meaning* of a word. For example: *bean, bin, Ben, ban, bun,* and *barn* are different in only one sound, the vowel sound between /b/ and /n/. Similarly, *bit, lit, knit,* and *sit* have only one sound difference, the initial consonant. (Note we are talking about *sounds,* not letters, so in phonemic terms the letters *kn* represent the single sound /n/.) The phonemes of different languages are rarely exactly the same, although many phonemes in the student's first language may be close. Most second language learners, especially in the early stages of learning the language, make use of the closest sound in their own language when the English phoneme is unfamiliar (and they probably "hear" it as the sound in their own language, too). For example, they may use the phoneme /s/ for the *th* sound at the beginning of words like *think* and *thing.* Or they may not be able to produce the distinction between some of the vowel sounds noted here. This is usually what is happening when we talk of someone having a "foreign accent." In reality, young children rarely continue to have problems with the pronunciation of English once they begin to become familiar with the language, and as Chapter 1 pointed out, many learners very quickly begin to sound like native speakers. In later life, although older learners have other advantages in learning a second language, this ability to learn a new set of phonemes decreases considerably.

Another aspect of spoken English that students may find hard to master is its stress system. In connected speech, many languages have equal stress on every syllable, whereas English stresses some syllables but not others. In <u>this</u> sentence, the <u>stressed</u> syllables are <u>marked</u>. Say that sentence and note how the underlined words receive more stress. Notice also how the vowel in the word *are* "weakens"—that is, it changes from the way it would be pronounced if you said it in isolation. Most "function words" or grammatical words change, or weaken, in this way, because they are not normally stressed in connected speech. Compare how you might say the following words in isolation and in a sentence, and notice how the vowels weaken. Be sure to speak as naturally as possible.

Was.	She was playing.
Have.	They have finished. (Probably further reduced to they've).
To.	Give it back to him.
From.	He's just got back from his holiday in Italy.

Sometimes you may feel it necessary to focus specifically on the sounds of English, and also on its stress and intonation patterns. The following activities provide some ways to provide this practice. Note that focusing on sounds is closely related to pronunciation practice.

✳ *Minimal Pair Exercises*

In these activities, the focus is on differentiating between pairs of words that differ only in one sound, such as the ones below (see Gibbons 1993). Give students a list of pairs of words (such as *three, tree; bin, bean; bin, pin; cat, cap; thing, sing*). They listen to *one* of the two words being read and circle on their list the one they think they hear. (For younger children, you could use two drawings rather than words.) Such exercises may be useful for some older learners who may find new sounds difficult to hear or to pronounce, and who are also likely to be more conscious of sounding "different," but in general, try to provide a greater contextualization for a task like this. After all, we rarely listen to words in isolation in real life, and, as we have seen, we use contextual clues to help us "hear" a sound correctly. You should also ask yourself these questions:

- Do these sounds make it difficult for the student to comprehend what is said to him or her?
- Does the student's pronunciation of these sounds actually make comprehension difficult for a listener?

If the answer is *no*, consider whether such exercises are really relevant. In any case, remember that such focused practice is better done regularly but in small doses, perhaps for a few minutes a day.

A more contextualized version of this activity is to locate the words the students are listening to within a whole text, focusing on minimal pairs of words. For example, students hear pairs of sentences like these:

1. A. On his way to market, Jack met an old man who offered to exchange Jack's cow for some bins.
    B. On his way to market, Jack met an old man who offered to exchange Jack's cow for some beans.

2. A. The beanstalk was as thick as a tree.
    B. The beanstalk was as sick as a tree.

The response sheet has *only* the number of the question, and the letters A and B. Children mark or circle the answer that they think they hear. Encourage them to think about the meaning too. For a small group of students, or individuals, it may be more effective to record the two versions, so that they have a chance to listen several times. Again, they mark the one that best makes sense.

✳ *Word Linking*

Learners also need to be able to recognize critical grammatical markers, such as past tense or plural endings. This may be difficult for some children who come from languages where final consonants are not fully "released." Many Asian speakers, for example, may have difficulties with the sounds /p/, /b/, /t/, /d/, /k/, /g/ in English when they occur at the end of a word. Learners' speech will be less "staccato-like" in these contexts if you get them to consciously link the end of one word with the beginning of the next. For example:

Get it out please.	Ge-ti-tout please.
Put it in the bin.	Pu-ti-tin the bin.
He said I could take it.	He sai-dI-could-ta-kit.

Jazz chants and poems are especially good for this activity. (Note that the sounds of English spoken in different parts of the world vary, and the letter *t* may be pronounced close to /d/ in parts of North America and Australia, but the "linking" principle described here remains.)

✳ *Say It Again*

This activity is adapted from Rost (1991), who suggests it for focusing on phonological features, stress, and intonation. First, select a scene from a video that the children will enjoy or find memorable, or that has high interest for them. This could be an excerpt from a children's television drama or feature film. Students should be familiar with the overall story line, so it would be better to use a video that they have previously watched.

Select some lines spoken by the characters in the video; these are the lines that students are later going to practice. The lines should be in chronological order but should not occur all together. Write the lines on a chart so there will be a whole-class focus on them. Next:

- Play the excerpt to the children.
- After they have watched the video, ask them to say the sentences on the chart. Ask if they can remember who said them, and where they occurred.
- Play the scene a second time while the students listen for the sentences. Have them raise their hand each time they hear one. Stop the tape at this point and ask them to repeat the line, *exactly* as it was said. Pay attention to all aspects of pronunciation, including stress, intonation, and vowel weakening. They may need several rehearsals with you!
- Play the scene a third time. This time, stop the tape before the selected lines. The students say the line as you point to it. After several repetitions, continue the tape until just before the next line. Encourage the students to say the lines in character, not simply to repeat them as an exercise.
- If students are enjoying the activity, play the tape once more and have individual students say the lines from memory.

✳ *Shadow Reading*

Tape a short story, and give students a copy of one paragraph. They first listen to the story all the way through. Then play only the paragraph, stopping after each sentence to give students a chance to repeat it. As for Say It Again, they should try to copy your pronunciation, stress, intonation, and pace as closely as possible. When the whole of the paragraph has been rehearsed in this way, students "shadow" the tape by reading along with it, remembering to pay attention to the stress and intonation patterns. This stage may be better done as individual work so that children can proceed at their own pace.

In Summary

As Rost (1991) points out, progress in listening provides a basis for the development of other language skills, and is involved in many language-learning activities. The activities in this chapter are based on a number of principles. Being aware of these may help in the design of other activities in your own classroom:

- Listening ability develops in both one-way and two-way contexts. There should be a balance of both in an effective listening program.
- Just as it is possible to read in more than one way (such as skimming and scanning), so it is possible to listen in different ways (such as for specific information or for overall gist). Again, teaching and learning activities should reflect these purposes.
- Learning to ask for clarification is integral to interactive listening.
- Noticing the form of words, being able to discriminate sounds, and being able to recognize stress and intonation patterns are part of learning to listen accurately. However, learners can often focus on these aspects of listening in the context of meaning-oriented activities.
- Listening ability develops where there is a real purpose for listening, and where the focus is on listening for meaning. And so, in the ESL context, the teaching of listening skills fits naturally into all curriculum areas. Designing listening tasks in the context of understanding and learning subject "content" provides authentic situations across the curriculum for listening skills to be developed.

And one final point. Becoming a good listener *yourself* is all-important. If we want children to become good listeners, we must ourselves become active listeners of what they say to us. Model effective listening by clarifying and checking that you have understood what children are saying. Reflect this back to them, and build on their responses as an interested conversational partner. This behavior demonstrates the importance you place on active listening, and it is one of the most positive ways you can develop your students' listening abilities.

Suggestions for Further Reading

NUNAN, D. 1990. "Learning to Listen in a Second Language." *Prospect* 5 (2): 7–23.

NUNAN, D., and L. MILLER, eds. 1995. *New Ways in Teaching Listening*. Alexandria, VA: Teachers of English to Speakers of Other Languages (TESOL).

ROST, M. 1991. *Listening in Action*. New York: Prentice Hall.

7

Learning Language, Learning Through Language, and Learning About Language
Developing an Integrated Curriculum

*What ESL learners are entitled to is the best available
environment for language and cognitive development.
Given the language-rich, child-centred quality of
kindergarten and primary [elementary] practice . . .
there is little doubt that in the early years of schooling,
the mainstream classroom forms the best basis for this.*
John Clegg, *Mainstreaming ESL: Case Studies in
Integrating ESL Students into the Mainstream
Curriculum*

The Curriculum: A Context for Language Learning

This chapter brings together the ideas in this book and discusses some of the ways in
which ESL teaching can be integrated into the regular classroom. Part of the title of
the chapter comes from a paper by Michael Halliday entitled "Three Aspects of Children's Language Development: Learning Language, Learning Through Language and
Learning About Language." These three aspects of language development are brought
together in a classroom program that integrates curriculum and language learning.

In the past, ESL teaching was often quite separate from whatever was going on in
the mainstream curriculum. Students followed a special program, for which they were
usually withdrawn from their classroom on a regular basis. This language program was
often organized around sets of grammatical structures (e.g., the present continuous
tense, the past tense, the present tense, prepositions, etc.) or around language functions (e.g., generalizing, classifying, hypothesizing, expressing time, expressing location,
etc.). Such approaches rely on the deliberate creation of contexts for using the language. For example, to practice the kinds of conditional language associated with
hypothesizing (such as *if we were . . . we would . . .*), a typical exercise might require
children to think of six items they would need if they were stranded on an island (the

118

assumption being that this would elicit language such as *we would need . . . we would take . . .*). While this may seem a communicative language learning task, in that the language is being used for some purpose, there may be no rationale as to why this is a particularly relevant or meaningful piece of language for children to be learning at that point in time. Nor may the task itself have anything to do with the particular subject learning in which children are engaged back in their regular classroom. And often in programs designed simply to teach language, there may be a sequence of such exercises where the somewhat artificial contexts and random choice of language items bear no relationship with each other, nor to what is being learned at that time in the mainstream curriculum.

Of course, for some newly arrived children, a short daily withdrawal program may still be valuable, provided that the focus language in these classes is related to the mainstream curriculum. Students new to the school and to English, or who are very shy or traumatized, may gain confidence and become familiar and comfortable with their new surroundings more easily in this way. It may also be less threatening for them to learn in a small group rather than in a whole class, and they will have many more opportunities to interact on a one-to-one basis with a teacher.

However, this chapter is based on the view that for most ESL learners, the regular classroom offers the best opportunity to learn a second language. In particular, the regular classroom provides a cultural and situational context for a focus on those aspects of the second language most relevant to curriculum learning.

Why Integrate?

Language teaching methodologies have generally accepted the notion that language teaching is more effective when learners are presented with meaningful language in context, and the integration of ESL learning with curriculum content is now broadly accepted as supportive of second language learning (Short 1993). There are a number of reasons why this is the approach taken here.

- First, the integration of language and content is consistent with the notion that language is learned through meaningful use in a variety of contexts. The subject matter of the curriculum provides those contexts, and thus a rationale for what language to teach. From a language-teaching perspective, then, the curriculum can be seen as providing authentic contexts for the development of subject-specific genres and registers. In short, an integrated program takes a functional approach to language and places its teaching focus on language as the medium of learning, rather than on language as something separate from content.
- Second, as discussed in Chapter 1, there is evidence that it can take between five and seven years for ESL students to match their English-speaking peers in the effective use of the academic registers of school. Clearly, if this is the case, concurrent teaching and learning of both subject matter and language is a way

of speeding up this process, and helping to ensure that children's classroom time is spent as usefully as possible.

- Third, nonintegrated approaches—instruction in language alone—is usually insufficient to enable children to succeed in mainstream studies (Adamson 1993; Richards and Hurley 1990; Collier 1995). As we noted earlier, if children are following a separate ESL program, there is a risk that there will be little relationship between the language being presented in the language class, and the language required for children to access and participate in curriculum learning. Since language is best learned in the service of other learning, the mainstream curriculum is an obvious source for language development: as one educator puts it, "Why go to the trouble of artificially recreating the mainstream classroom [in withdrawal classes] when the real thing is available next door?" (Clegg 1996, 10).

- In addition, situating language teaching within a curriculum area has the potential to support both language and curriculum learning, in a reciprocal way. With a dual content-language focus, there is likely to be a continuous recycling of concepts, grammar, or vocabulary associated with particular curriculum knowledge. As we saw in Chapter 5, prior knowledge or familiarity with a topic greatly facilitates language comprehension and language learning. Equally, language-based tasks in a subject area can effectively recycle particular curriculum concepts and knowledge in the process of focusing on relevant text types, registers, grammar, and vocabulary. In other words, "the curriculum is the hook on which to hang language development and vice versa" (Clegg 1996, 15).

- Finally, it is important to recognize the benefits to all students of a culturally and linguistically diverse classroom, and a culturally inclusive and language-aware curriculum. As Clegg (1996) points out, "the language-rich diet of an ESL group can turn out to be nourishing for the whole mainstream class. It can help all the children use language for learning in ways which were not previously available to them" (12). We should recognize that separate provision for ESL students impoverishes the school as a whole: it reinforces monoculturalism and puts the school at odds with the reality of the culturally diverse society in which it is situated. In the world of the twenty-first century, all children will increasingly need, as one writer puts it, to "navigate difference."

As we pointed out in Chapter 1, however, merely placing children in the mainstream classroom does not ensure they will learn the language of instruction. Good content teaching is not necessarily good language teaching, and at the same time, subject teaching must go beyond the concerns of the language specialist. An integrated program takes a functional approach to language, systematically relating it to the uses of language in the curriculum, so that curriculum topics will have both subject and specific language aims. When this occurs, the curriculum can provide an authentic context for meaningful and purposeful language use. There are a range of ways in which integration has been interpreted and organized (for excellent summaries of these, see Davison and Williams 2001, 58–59; and Clegg 1996, 22). This chapter offers a further example of how this integration can occur.

Integrating Language and Subject Learning: What Do We Need to Know First?

In this section we'll look at the kind of information that needs to be gathered prior to actual classroom planning. There are two sets of information that form the basis for the planning of a program that integrates second language learning and curriculum learning. They are the responses to these two questions:

- What are the language demands of the curriculum?
- What do children currently know about language, and what are their language-learning needs?

The first question requires "finding the language" in the subjects and topics that children are studying. The second requires finding out about children's current language abilities. In the following two sections, we'll look at each of these areas.

Finding the Language in the Curriculum

First, think about the topics or units of work that you are currently working with in your classroom program. Examples of "topics" or "unit of work" could be: our neighborhood, small creatures, electricity, the water cycle, a local issue, producing a class paper, making a school garden, symmetry and patterning, designing a kite.

Most teachers are accustomed to thinking about planning for subject learning in terms of the content, tasks, and resources they will use, and program objectives are frequently thought of in terms of subject learning. Although most teachers are aware of the importance of language in the classroom, it is often not explicitly planned for across the curriculum. The temptation is to look "through" language to the content. Figure 7–1 provides a series of questions designed to help you think about the *language* that is integral to a particular curriculum topic. These questions are not intended to be definitive. Nor is it suggested that you take account of every question in every unit of work. Rather, they are intended to prompt you to think about your program through the "lens" of language, to help you hold language up to the light, to look *at* it rather than *through* it.

The questions aim to do two things. First, they aim to help you identify the language demands of a particular topic or area of study, and to determine what language children would need to know in order to participate in learning in that curriculum topic. Second, they aim to help you identify if and where opportunities for language development are being missed, such as to draw attention to a missed opportunity to develop listening skills. Each set of questions is headed with a reference to the chapter

See Chapters 2 & 3	*See Chapter 6*	*See Chapter 5*	*See Chapter 4*	*See Chapters 2, 3, & 5*	*See Chapters 2, 3, & 5*
What spoken language demands will there be?	What listening tasks will there be?	What texts will students be reading?	What are the written text types that will occur, or what text types could be included?	What aspects of grammar (e.g, tense) does the topic require students to use?	What specific vocabulary does the topic require students to know?
If there are currently not many opportunities for spoken language, where can oral tasks be included?	What kind of listening do they involve: one-way? two-way? interpersonal? transactional?	What are the possible linguistic and cultural barriers students may encounter?	What is the schematic structure of these text types?		
	If there are currently not many listening tasks, what specific listening activities could be included?	How can texts be made accessible to students?	What kind of connectives occur in these text types?		
		Do reading tasks aim to increase readers' reading strategies, and students' knowledge about language?	If there are few written tasks, what text types would be relevant and could be included?		
		If there are few reading texts, are there others that could be included?			

FIGURE 7–1. *Finding the Language in the Curriculum*

in which the particular issues are dealt with. You may wish to add other questions of your own.

Figure 7–2 is a worked example of the kinds of responses you might make to these questions. The topic is "A Local Issue," and it is adapted from a program from Creenaune and Rowles (1996). Creenaune and Rowles give the following as examples of local issues that have relevance to students' lives: aircraft noise under a flight path, a proposed local development in an environmentally sensitive area, demolition of a historic building, the preservation of an endangered species, the threatened closure of an important community service or facility, a campaign to improve local facilities for young people. Creenaune and Rowles include the following objectives for this unit:

> after thorough examination of all the arguments surrounding an issue, students will be encouraged to develop an informed position with supporting arguments and express this position in authentic forums, for example, writing to a newspaper or to local politicians, speaking at a school assembly or producing articles for the school maga-zine. (43–47)

In Figure 7–2, the left-hand column is a selection of the planned teaching and learning activities that would be included in such a topic. (Details of the particular issue have not been included since this would depend on the local situation.) The right-hand column "unpacks" these to identify what language knowledge and use is required in order to carry them out. It thus represents a "language inventory"—the language that is integral to planned teaching activities—and answers the first of the questions raised earlier: what are the language demands of the curriculum?

We will return to this language inventory later. At this point, let's turn to the sec-ond major question: what do children currently know about language, and what are their language-learning needs? This is the subject of the next section.

Finding Out About Children's Language

The second set of information focuses on the current language abilities of the chil-dren—what they are already able to do with language and the areas in which they need help. This is the information that effective language assessment practices pro-vide. Central to the notion of assessment here is the principle that the information it provides should be used to inform subsequent teaching and learning activities, and that it is an ongoing process that occurs in the context of the everyday activities of the classroom. It aims ultimately to support learning, not—as may be a risk with stan-dardized tests—to "legitimize the location of the 'problem' within students" (Cummins 2000).

Though there may be a place at times for the kind of information that standard-ized tests are able to provide, probably the most useful language assessment for teach-ers is that which provides information about children's mastery of the language of the classroom, in particular when it indicates the areas in which they currently require

Planned Teaching and Learning Activities	Finding the Language
Brainstorm what children know about issue and record ideas	Vocabulary for topic
Get information: write to key people or organizations to request information	Letters of request Use of politeness forms: *We would be grateful if . . .* *Could you please . . .*
Collect and read pamphlets, newspaper articles, or other published material and make notes	Skimming and scanning skills Summarizing Notetaking
Visit site/display areas and write a recount of the visit	Writing a recount Use of past tense Use of appropriate connectives (of time): *first, next, afterwards, finally*
Interview or invite key people to the school to speak about the issue from their perspective	Formulating questions for interview Asking the interviewee questions in an appropriate manner
Share all information with peers	Giving an oral report Listening skills: listening for key information
Examine similarities and differences between viewpoints of stakeholders	Use of comparison and contrast: *X argues . . . whereas Y argues . . .*
Small-group class discussions	Voicing disagreement politely: *I don't fully agree with you, in my opinion* Presenting opinions: *I'd like to say, I'd like to add, in my opinion* Using appropriate connectives for supporting arguments: *first, second, finally*
Address school assembly or other classes about the issue	Presenting an oral report • Using appropriate schematic structure • Presentation skills
Write letters to the local newspaper or articles for school newspaper presenting opinions	Writing an argument Use of appropriate schematic structure Use of appropriate connectives for presenting arguments: *first, second, therefore, in conclusion*

FIGURE 7–2. *A Significant Local Issue: A Language "Inventory"*

support. This kind of assessment is intended to *be ongoing and formative*, not to "place" children in relation to each other or be used as a summative "test." The aim is to provide you with useful information about the current language development of children that in turn will feed into subsequent teaching and learning activities. Such ongoing assessment is by its nature context specific, and so it will indicate to the teacher the level and kind of scaffolding that is most relevant for particular tasks.

Ongoing classroom assessment can occur in a number of ways, many of them informal, and many of which you probably already use. They include:

- Your observation of how children work and interact with others, such as how far they make use of environmental print around the room, their level of interest in reading and writing, and how confident they are in speaking.
- Your interaction with individual children, such as talking with them about how they have gone about solving a problem, listening to how they have reasoned a math task, discussing their understanding of what they are reading.
- The outcomes of listening, reading, speaking, and writing tasks.
- Portfolios of work.
- Children's own self-assessments.

All of these are valuable in helping build up a profile of a learner's language use.

It is also useful to carry out more systematic analyses of the language children actually produce when they speak and write; this information is especially important for the planning of an integrated program. The section on assessment in Chapter 4 is an example of how this can be done. It describes how children's writing can be assessed against criteria that are specific to a particular text type. In the same way, any learning task in which children are involved—including every activity described in the Glossary—can simultaneously be an assessment task. Here are two further examples of how regular classroom activities can be used as a means of assessing what children are able to do and where they need support. (For additional examples, see Gibbons 1992.)

ASSESSMENT TASK FOR SPEAKING: PAIRED PROBLEM SOLVING

One activity described in Chapter 2 was **paired problem solving.** The task requires students to work in pairs to solve one of two problems (the examples given in Chapter 2 were to design a paper boat that would keep afloat twenty marbles, and to design a mobile). Having come to a solution, two pairs cross-question each other about their solutions to their respective problems, prior to solving the second problem themselves. If this activity were also to be used as an assessment task, note that the aim would be to focus on the *language* involved in doing the task, rather than on the "best" solution to the problem. With this in mind, let's consider the kinds of criteria you may want to apply to evaluate what counts as a "successful" performance. (Note that assessment of children's spoken language is easier if the talk is audiotaped. This can also be played back to children as a way of having them reflect on their own performance.)

First, think about what this task requires children to be able to do, in linguistic terms. It requires them to describe their problem, and then to report their solution. The reporting will require them to use the past tense, to use appropriate vocabulary (e.g., *tore, broke, fell apart, sunk, floated, flat-bottomed, pointed*), and to give reasons for the various solutions they have tried (e.g., *We did that because we thought . . .*). The task will also require children to ask appropriate questions about the other pair's problem and solution (e.g., *So, what happened? What did you do then?*). And, as a significant part of the task, it will require them to give advice appropriately (e.g., *You could . . . Have you tried . . . –ing? Do you think you should have . . . ? Perhaps it would be better if . . .*). And it is likely that they will also need to be able to acknowledge this advice (e.g., *That's a good idea; We could try that; No, I don't think that will work because . . .*).

Of course, what you are doing when you "unpack" a task in this way is also an example of "finding the language in the curriculum," and you may wish to take account of this in your classroom planning. Used as an assessment procedure, these examples of task-related language can be translated into a set of criteria by which a learner's language can be assessed. Figure 7–3 is a worked example of this and illustrates how one child (Mario) was assessed.

At the same time, it's important to note that if a learner doesn't fulfill one of these criteria, it does not necessarily indicate an *inability* to use language in this way. For example, let's say the child did not offer advice to the other pair. This only shows that, in this context, the learner didn't indicate whether or not he or she could offer advice. Perhaps the child simply chose not to. So it is important not to overgeneralize about learners' abilities on the basis of context-specific tasks.

On the other hand, if assessment is an ongoing process and takes into account a range of contexts in which learners use language, such assessment procedures gradually build up to form a profile of how learners use language in the classroom. The assessment in Figure 7–3 indicates that Mario was able to report what he and his partner did, but had difficulty in using the kind of modulation by which English speakers offer advice: *you could . . . it might be better if . . . maybe you should . . .* and so forth.

ASSESSMENT TASK FOR READING: CLOZE EXERCISE

There are many ways to assess reading, and many resources and books available on the subject. It is beyond the scope of this chapter to discuss reading assessment in detail. Popular ways of assessing children include using anecdotal records, miscue analysis, reading conferences, children's own reading logs, audiotapes of oral readings, teacher-student conferences, and retelling or rewriting what has been read (see Earnest Garcia 1994). As in the previous example for assessing spoken language, the purpose here is simply to show how a regular teaching activity can be used for the purpose of assessment.

Since it has been mentioned several times in this book, we will look at how **cloze** activities can be used in this way. Cloze tests were originally developed to reflect the theory that reading entails the prediction of what will come next, and were discussed as teaching (rather than testing) procedures in Chapter 5, and in the Glossary. Again,

Criteria	NAME: Mario
Was the learner able to . . .	**Comments**
Describe the problem	Was able to do this quite clearly.
Report their solution: - Use the past tense - Use appropriate vocabulary - Give reasons for actions	Made some past tense mistakes ("try," "putted") but meaning was clear. Vocabulary limited but showed good strategies for making meaning—"boat was not point at bottom" (flat-bottomed?) Not demonstrated
Ask appropriate questions	Asked mainly WH questions. Question forms sometimes inaccurate—"how you did?" "why you do that?"
Offer advice appropriately	Used "maybe" throughout—"maybe you try like this." No other use of modality (e.g., you could have . . .). Overall communicated this well.
Acknowledge advice	Not demonstrated
Other comments	Mario participated very actively in this activity—much more confident now—maybe because he felt he really had something to say. Focus LANGUAGE AREAS: tense, question forms, modality

FIGURE 7–3.   *Example of Task Assessment: Shared Problem Solving*

while regular deletions throughout the text (for example, every sixth or seventh word) may give general information about a reader's overall understanding of the text, a well-constructed cloze with selective deletions can give you more specific information about children's reading strategies. It can tell you about what kinds of strategies children are using to gain meaning from text, such as using backward referencing (using the preceding text to find a clue) or forward referencing (looking ahead in the text to find a clue). Children who are unable to use backward and forward referencing will read word by word, and they will probably be unable to carry meaning within or across sentences.

Cloze activities can also be used to focus on whether a learner understands critical grammatical markers, such as connectives that link ideas and signal the logical development of a text. A cloze exercise based on an argument or discussion text (see Chapter 4) could be used for this purpose. In this case, grammatical deletions would include the logical connectives in the text, such as *first, second, finally, on the other hand, however, therefore.*

A few words of warning, however. First, as we have seen, the process of reading depends greatly on the reader's current level of knowledge of the topic, and familiarity with the type of genre. If your aim is to assess a child's comprehension ability to process text, then ensure that for assessment purposes the topic and genre are familiar ones, so that as far as possible you are focusing on the child's linguistic understandings (rather than on possible "gaps" in the child's cultural or world knowledge in relation to the text). Second, remember that at least the first and last sentences of a cloze exercise should be complete, since without these the reader has an unrealistic reading task, in being required to understand a text that lacks a clear context.

Planning a Unit That Integrates Language and Curriculum Learning

At this point you have made a "language inventory" of what the topic will require children to be able to do—the linguistic demands that will be made on them—and you have a considerable amount of information through ongoing formal and informal assessment about what children are currently able to do (including some of the areas where they still need support). These two sets of information form the basis of an integrated program. Before discussing its development, I will reiterate some key pedagogical principles for promoting second language learners' linguistic and cognitive development, and the growth of critical literacy skills.

Cummins (2000) suggests three interrelated areas as critical to such a pedagogy:

1. *A focus on meaning.* This requires input, or the language that children listen to or read, to be comprehensible. It also includes the development of critical literacy.
2. *A focus on language.* This includes the development of children's awareness of language forms and uses, and the ability to critically analyze these.

3. *A focus on use*. This involves using language to transform what has been learned, through generating new knowledge, creating literature and art, and acting on social realities.

Integral to each of these—and congruent with the socio-cultural view of learning that informs the discussion throughout this book—is the acknowledgment that student learning is inseparable from the interactions between teachers and learners.

A Framework for Planning

The framework for planning an integrated unit takes these principles into account, and it also draws on the earlier discussion relating to the language demands of the curriculum and the language needs of the children (see Figure 7–4). The framework is intended to provide an ESL focus to a mainstream program, and to be a supplement to your normal program, not to replace it. In addition, it is intended to fulfill two purposes:

1. To facilitate joint planning, where two teachers—an ESL teacher and a classroom teacher—plan and/or teach a class collaboratively.
2. To help a classroom teacher who is working alone to plan systematically for the needs of the second language learners in her class.

The framework in Figure 7–4 has been partially completed for an upper elementary class studying the "local issue" topic discussed earlier. (For a similar example with a younger class, see Gibbons 1993.) The particular issue for this class was centered around the local park, which also had a swimming pool that many of the children visited regularly. A proposal had been put forward by the local council to develop part of the park space as a multistory parking lot to serve the local shopping area. Community feeling was split over this, and the local newspaper at the time was a source for letters both supporting and opposing the development, and for articles and editorials. Other material included a plan of the proposed development at the local library, and the local council newsletter.

BOXES A AND B: STUDENT NEEDS AND CURRICULUM DEMANDS

Box A summarizes the information about the students gained from ongoing assessment, and Box B represents the language inventory for the topic (see Figure 7–2 for a summary of the planned teaching activities). It should be noted, though, that not all the needs identified through assessment can be addressed at once! Indeed, the nature of the topic may mean that it is not the appropriate vehicle to focus on some language areas. For example, although narrative structure has been identified in this class as an area of difficulty, this topic is probably not going to provide an authentic context for that to be a relevant language focus at this point in time. Integration cannot be forced:

A. Students' Language Development Needs

B. Language Inventory (language demands of the topic)

- discussion genre (organizational structure, connectives, and conjunctions)
- narrative genre (organizational structure, use of <u>past tense</u>)
- reading for key information
- listening for key information
- asking for clarification
- making suggestions
- giving opinions, expressing agreement and disagreement
- questioning

- skim and scan for key information (readers' letters, articles in local newspaper)
- take part in small-group discussions (sample language: *could you explain that, I don't agree that . . ., in my opinion . . .*)
- construct accurate and appropriate questions (for questionnaire)
- recount of site visit
- discussion genre
- oral reports to other classes
- key vocabulary: *pedestrian, facility, recreation, issue, community, traffic flow . . .*

C. Activities to Develop Focus Language

- Joint construction of recount (based on site visit), focus on past tense, time connectives, vocabulary
- Wallpaper Brainstorm to elicit ideas for and against development
- Jigsaw Reading, using range of letters to local newspaper, focus on skimming and scanning for key information
- Dictogloss (use simplified editorial as text)
- Hot Seat: visitor from five years in the future, advantages and disadvantages of development
- Find the Difference (for lower-level ESL students), pictures before and after development, to focus on vocabulary
- Curriculum Cycle for teaching discussion genre (use cloze, text reconstruction, and split dictation to model the text type)

D. Evaluation

FIGURE 7–4.   *A Framework for the Integration of Language and Content*

if a particular text type or grammatical item has not been identified in your language inventory, it is better to address that particular area of language in another unit. It is likely, however, that the "local issue" topic will provide authentic contexts for some of the areas identified as children's language learning needs. Links have been drawn to indicate these areas of "match." They include:

- The structure of written discussions.
- The use of connectives and conjunctions within this text type (presenting an opinion in a letter to the editor of a local paper).
- Skimming and scanning skills (in reading relevant pamphlets or informational material).
- Summarizing information.
- Listening for key information.
- Giving opinions and expressing agreement and disagreement.

These areas, then, have been chosen as the language focuses for this topic because they are both relevant to the needs of the children *and* congruent with the language demands of the topic.

BOX C: DEVELOPING THE FOCUS LANGUAGE

The next decision is how to develop this focus language. Box C lists the particular language tasks that are intended to model the focus language and to give opportunities for students to use it. All the activities listed here have been introduced throughout the book and are listed in the Glossary, but you will probably be able to think of others. These activities are the means by which the focus language is translated into meaningful teaching and learning activities that are relevant both to the language needs of the students *and* to the topic being studied.

Box C thus represents:

- The scaffolding by which learners are helped to access the language identified in Box B.
- The means by which teachers can respond to some of the language needs identified in Box A, in the context of the mainstream curriculum.
- The language focus for the unit.

BOX D: EVALUATION

Box D is the evaluation of the unit. There may be many things you wish to evaluate: for example, the resources used, students' enjoyment of the unit, their ability to work collaboratively, and the relevance and design of the tasks, as well as what students have learned. Again, the framework is not intended to replace this broad evaluation, simply to add to it. The information Box D contains will reflect the initial identification of children's language-learning needs and the demands of the curriculum—that is, it relates to what has been identified in Box A and Box B. Broadly, in this unit, it will address questions such as whether or not the children are now better able to:

- Structure an argument.
- Use appropriate connectives to present ideas in an argument.
- Skim and scan for information.
- Summarize information.

Consider also the issues raised in Chapter 1 about the need for appropriate scaffolding and choice of tasks. In reflecting on your own role as a teacher, ask yourself these questions:

- Did the program build on and link to what children already know?
- Did teaching and learning tasks sufficiently extend learners beyond what they could already do?
- Was adequate and appropriate scaffolding provided so that tasks could be successfully completed?
- Is there evidence that children have developed new concepts or reached new levels of understanding, such that they will be able to use these in new contexts and for their own purposes?

Phonics, Spelling, and Grammar: Where Do They Fit in an Integrated Unit?

The final sections of this chapter address a number of related questions that concern many teachers, particularly those who are committed to teaching language in ways that recognize its wholeness and see it as a system for meaning making. Many teachers ask themselves:

- Is it still relevant to focus on phonics, spelling, and grammar?
- Is it possible to focus on them within an integrated meaning-focused approach?

To both these questions, my own response would be *yes*: as most teachers would agree, there is a place for the teaching of phonics, spelling, and grammar—in other words, for a focus on language as "object." There is a place for children to learn *about* language, as well as to learn it and to learn through it. The critical question, of course, is how this can be done in ways that do not compromise interactive and meaning-driven classroom practices.

It is useful to bear in mind three principles:

1. Move from whole to part.
2. Move from meaning to form.
3. Move from familiar to unfamiliar.

And, for all three principles, we should add "and back again"! To form a metaphor for these principles, imagine yourself standing on a hillside looking out across a panoramic view, with a pair of binoculars in your hand. In front of you are fields, mountains, and forests. In the far distance, you can glimpse the sea and a boat. Your first gaze is at the whole vista ahead of you, the overall view from where you are standing. But after a while, you use your binoculars to focus in on a particular part of the view, to hone in on a detail of the landscape. (You know how to locate this detail, where to train your binoculars, because you have already seen it as a part of the whole.) When you have finished focusing on these details you will probably savor the whole panorama again, but this time with an enhanced sense of what is there.

In this scenario, what you almost certainly would *not* do is look through the binoculars before you have first looked at the view and located an area to focus on. Neither would you turn around and point the binoculars behind you! (Because, of course, if you did either of these things, you wouldn't really know what you were looking at.)

To return this idea to the classroom, imagine the topic you are working on to be the view. Your overall aim is for students to construct knowledge and develop understandings about the topic, and to use language meaningfully and purposefully. But this does not prevent you, in the course of the topic, from "training the binoculars" by helping your students focus "close up" on a detail of language: a point of grammar, some phonic knowledge, a spelling pattern, the schematic structure of a particular genre, or a group of connectives and conjunctions. (Remember, you have already identified these through the language inventory of the topic and through what you know about students' language needs.) You may wish to spend some time on this "close-up view," but while you are doing so both you and the students know where these "parts" fit into the "whole," and how the focus on form is related to the meanings being made. Approaching the teaching of forms and parts in this way puts grammar, spelling, and phonics where they belong: as worthy objects of study in the service of meaning making and learning. In other words, learning about language is most meaningful when it occurs in the context of language-in-use. Figure 7–5 illustrates this idea.

The "hourglass" here illustrates how the focus of teaching and learning changes throughout the teaching of a topic, with the "narrowing" of the hourglass representing a focus on language itself. Teaching and learning activities move at times from learning *through* language, to learning *about* language, to once more learning *through* language. In other words, teaching progresses from meaning to form, from whole to part, and back again. The focus on "language as object" is in the context of the overall

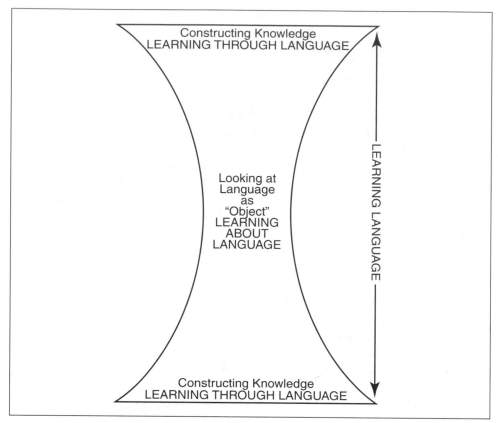

FIGURE 7–5. *Focusing on Language as "Object"*

meanings being made and the curriculum knowledge being constructed. As discussed earlier, the choice of what aspects of grammar, spelling, or phonic knowledge to focus on will already have been determined by the choice of language focus for the topic, but it may be that in the course of the unit of work, you will have identified other language aspects of the topic that you wish to address.

Teaching Phonemic Awareness and Spelling: Recognizing Analogies

Some researchers have shown a strong relationship between children's awareness of phonemic patterns (the relationships between sounds and letters) and their ability to rhyme (see Bryant and Bradley 1985; Goswani and Bryant 1990). Children's rhyming skills appear to be good predictors of later spelling and reading success. A child who is good at rhyming may realize that shared sounds between words, such as *hat* and *rat*, often also mean shared spelling patterns. Later on, they may work out how to recognize or spell a word that they have not seen before through analogies with more familiar words. (For example, knowing how to read or spell *light* may help them read or spell *fright*.) Being able to form *generalizations* about how words are read or spelled, through *analogy,* is a reasoning process that is essential for developing phonemic awareness in reading and recognition of orthography (spelling patterns) in writing.

The use of rhymes and books containing rhyme are likely to be helpful for all children learning to read and write. Being able to recognize words that rhyme and to be helped to produce rhymes is probably especially useful for children who are less familiar with the sounds of the language. (At the same time, note that books containing large numbers of "nonsense" rhyming words may initially be very confusing for ESL learners.)

The teaching of phonemic awareness (knowledge of letter-sound relationships) and spelling is usually seen as of particular significance for younger grades, although many older ESL learners may also need a specific focus on these aspects of language too. Once again, the principles of whole to part, and familiar to unfamiliar, are important ones.

TEACHING PHONEMIC AWARENESS

An alphabetic system uses letters as symbols for sounds, so that it is possible for a reader to use letter-sound relationships in decoding words. As discussed in Chapter 5, this is one of several reading strategies that children need to acquire. However, in English, letter-sound relationships do not always help, since they are not always consistent. Children therefore need to become aware that letter-sound relationships lead to possibilities, rather than certainties! Learning about phonic generalizations can help children in two ways:

1. When readers meet a word they do not know, one of several strategies they need to use is checking their prediction against the first letter or letter cluster of the word (see Chapter 5). Phonic knowledge is essential for this.
2. Sometimes it is possible for an unknown word to be "sounded out" by the reader. If the word is already known aurally, this process may allow the reader to recognize the word.

However, letters and sounds in isolation are very abstract concepts, even for native speakers, and introducing individual letters, letter clusters, or blends out of a meaningful context is an even more abstract task for a student who is unfamiliar with the language and the sounds of the language. Therefore, as a general approach, embed any focus on phonics teaching within familiar material that is meaningful to the learner. A Big Book that has been read several times is a useful vehicle for phonics teaching. The following process provides one example of a simplified procedure to use with beginning readers that illustrates how phonemic awareness can be developed inductively, using the three principles of moving from known to unknown, from whole to part, and from meaning to form. (You would probably want to add other related activities as well.)

- Choose a book that you have already read several times with children (and with which they can now probably join in as you read). Select a sentence relevant to the phonic knowledge you want to focus on. Read it together with the children, pointing to the words as you read. For example: *Run, run, as fast as you can; you can't catch me, I'm the gingerbread man!*
- From the sentence, select a word containing the relevant letters and sounds you wish to focus on. Here you may select the word *man*. Read it with the children. Ask individual children to point to it within the sentence, or find it in the book.
- Use the word *man* to generate other *–an* words. They may be others in the same book (*can*) or ones children already know (*ran*) or that can be easily illustrated (*pan*).
- Read the book again, asking children to point to any *–an* words.
- Make up wall charts with lists of these words, and encourage children to add to them as they find or think of new words. These words may come from other books, wall charts, or words already known to the children. These specific words can be used to help children come to a generalization about the way in which the sound common to all is written down. Gradually introduce more complex words that illustrate the same sound-letter relationship (*hand, land, sand*).

What is important here is that children learn about sound-letter relationships inductively, within the context of something that is meaningful and whole, rather than through abstract and unrelated phonics exercises. There may be times when a more deductive approach is useful. Children who are already literate in their first language may appreciate being given a generalization explicitly and finding other examples. (This is the approach taken in many phonic-driven approaches to the teaching of reading.) But this becomes a "telling" rather than a "reasoning" process.

TEACHING ABOUT SPELLING

The phrase "teaching *about* spelling" is used in place of "teaching spelling" deliberately here, to emphasize again that—as with learning phonic knowledge—learning to spell is largely a reasoning process and one based on the learner's ability to develop generalizations. Once the child has discovered that written words are constant and can be named, then, as discussed earlier, the sounds of the words can be related to the letters that represent the words. But it is probably as children begin to find a way to represent what they want to write themselves that they need to explore more systematically how the phonemic system works.

It is important to recognize that the phonetic spellings of a young learner are often indicative of positive understandings about the systems of orthography (spelling patterns) of English; *train* written as *chrn*, *elephant* written as *elft*, or *shopping* written as *shpg* indicate that quite a lot has been learned about sound-letter relationships. The unconventional spellings used by children in the earlier stages of writing are usually quite systematic and related to the way they are articulating the words. Breaking up words into their constituent sounds is not an easy matter, especially for an ESL learner.

One of the major ways that children learn to spell is to recognize and reproduce common spelling patterns. Collecting and recording words that have a common pattern and that rhyme is one way of doing this (see Figure 7–6 as examples). Encourage children to add to these lists as they find new words with the same pattern.

When children do not know the spelling of a word, try to scaffold *how* to spell:

- Encourage children to "have a go" at writing a word, to use their existing knowledge about how sounds are written.
- Encourage them to articulate the word slowly, and as they say the word, to think about each of the sounds they can hear.

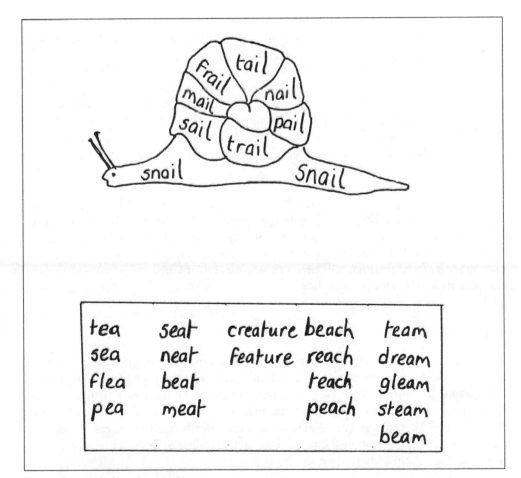

FIGURE 7–6. *Finding Common Patterns*

- Draw analogies with other known words, and help them recognize a common pattern.

Note that providing lists of *thematically* related words to be learned by rote (perhaps related to a topic being studied) may assist in the learning of new vocabulary, but it may *not* be helpful in teaching *about* spelling, since thematically related words are unlikely to have a spelling pattern in common.

In Summary

In this chapter, we have looked at a number of reasons for supporting the integration of ESL students into the mainstream class:

- Language is best learned through meaningful use in a variety of contexts, and the curriculum is an ideal and ready-made resource for a focus on language for learning.
- Concurrent teaching of language and content allows ESL students to continue learning as they are developing their second language
- Language and curriculum learning support each other via the ongoing recycling of concepts and knowledge and the language through which they are expressed.
- The "language-rich diet" of ESL teaching is of benefit to all students: it supports all children to use language in ways that are new and critical to academic learning.

In an integrated curriculum, children learn language, learn through language, and learn about language. They *learn* language in the process of using it. They learn *through* language when they use it to construct knowledge across all areas of the curriculum. And they learn *about* language when there is a focus on "language as object." In a well-planned integrated program, all three of these aspects of language development have the potential to be brought together.

A Final Word

The potential for learning is not finite or bounded. And the potential for learning in school should not be restricted by a student's lack of knowledge of the language of instruction, because in this case—to return to the conclusion of Chapter 1—ESL learners are denied their right to be full members of the school community. They should not be expected to "prove themselves linguistically before they can claim their full entitlement." The responsibility for their second language development belongs to the school and ultimately to their teachers.

No matter the educational constraints on both teachers and students sometimes imposed by government policies or education systems, *individual* teachers can and do make a difference to children's lives. The notion of scaffolding that has been a recurrent theme throughout this book represents a way that individual teachers can maintain high expectations of their students and reject the inequality that offers to some students an alternative or watered-down curriculum, or one that, for reasons of language, they are unable to access. It assumes three principles. The first is to link with and build on what children bring to school: their language, culture, understandings, and experiences. The second is to provide the kind of support—responsive to the particular language development needs of second language learners and to the language demands of the mainstream curriculum—to enable them to learn successfully through collaboration with their teachers and with other students. The third is the willingness to "hand over" to students the responsibility to use what they have learned independently, in new contexts and for their own purposes.

We know that some students begin their school life with less of what Delpit (1988) refers to as "the accoutrements of the culture of power" than other students. Some critical theorists refer to this as "cultural capital," and part of that cultural capital is the ability to control the spoken and written codes of the dominant society. As we have discussed, it would be wrong to assume that children who are not fluent in these codes will automatically acquire them through the process of being in school, without specific kinds of support. In the words of Julianna, with which this book began, ESL learners need to be able to use English not only for day-to-day purposes but "for school work and strangers"—for academic learning and ultimately for negotiating their place in the wider society. This book has suggested some ways in which individual teachers can help ensure that this occurs.

Suggestions for Further Reading

CLEGG, J., ed. 1996. *Mainstreaming ESL: Case Studies in Integrating ESL Students into the Mainstream Curriculum.* Clevedon, UK: Multilingual Matters. (See especially Introduction.)

CUMMINS, J. 2000. "Transformative Pedagogy: Who Needs It?" Chapter 10 in *Language, Power and Pedagogy: Bilingual Children in the Crossfire,* ed. J. Cummins. Clevedon, UK: Multilingual Matters.

DAVISON, C., and A. WILLIAMS. 2001. "Integrating Language and Content: Unresolved Issues." Chapter 3 in *English as a Second Language in the Mainstream: Teaching Learning and Identity,* ed. B. Mohan, C. Leung, and C. Davison. London: Longman.

SHORT, D. 1993. "Assessing Integrating Language and Content." *TESOL Quarterly* 27 (4): 627–56.

Glossary of Teaching Activities

Note: Where activities are described fully in the chapters, only a brief description is given here.

✳ *After-Reading Activities*

These activities include the following: story innovation; innovating on the ending; cartoon strip; readers' theatre; wanted posters; story map; time lines; hot seat; freeze frames; cloze; monster cloze; vanishing cloze; text reconstruction; consonant groups; phonic families; true/false questions; questioning the text. See Chapter 5.

✳ *Aural Cloze*

This is a cloze exercise that focuses on listening skills. Each student has a text with deletions. The full text is read aloud by the teacher and students must fill in the gaps. See Chapter 6.

✳ *Barrier Games*

Barrier games are discussed in detail in Chapter 2, along with other communicative games. They are usually played in pairs, and involve solving a problem of some sort. They involve an "information gap," whereby each player has different information that both need if they are to solve the problem. A feature of these games is that players should not be able to see the other player's information—hence the notion of a "barrier" between them. See also Chapter 4.

✳ *Before-Reading Activities*

These activities include the following: predicting from words; predicting from the title or first sentence; predicting from a key illustration; picture sequencing; reader questions; storytelling; storytelling in the mother tongue; sharing existing knowledge. See Chapter 5.

✳ *Cloze*

Cloze activities are pieces of text with some words deleted. They are a useful teaching strategy for encouraging students to use prediction skills as they are reading, to help you assess their general comprehension, and to gauge the difficulty of a text for a particular student. They can be based on a text students have already read, or they can be based on another familiar topic. Students should not be asked to do a cloze around a topic they know nothing about. See Chapter 5.

✳ *Describe and Draw*

This is a barrier game in which each child in a pair takes it in turns to describe something he or she is drawing (or has drawn). His or her partner then has to draw the same thing. See Chapter 2.

✳ *Dialogue Journal*

As the name suggests, this is a conversation that is written down. It may be between the student and teacher, or between an ESL student and an English-speaking buddy. See Figure G–1.

What did you do yesterday, Mario?

I go beek beets.

What did you do at the beach?

at the beach I swimmin.

Do you like swimming?
YES I like
Do you like a swimming

Yes I enjoy it very much, Mario!

FIGURE G–1. *Dialogue Journal*

* **Dictogloss**

This is a technique adapted from Ruth Wajnryb (1990). It is designed to develop listening skills, but is particularly valuable because it integrates this with speaking, reading, and writing.

1. The teacher reads a short passage twice (or more) at normal speed. The passage should be on a topic the students already know something about. (You could write the passage yourself, or you could use a passage from one of the students' textbooks in any curriculum area, or from a book related to a topic they are studying.) The students just listen; they don't write anything at this point.
2. The teacher reads the passage a third time at normal speed, and this time, while the teacher is reading, the students write down as much as they can, as fast as they can. They should not try to write sentences, just key words and phrases. It is important that you make clear to the students that you do not expect them to write everything down. The aim is just to get as much information as they can. Handwriting and spelling are not important at this stage.
3. In pairs, the students compare and discuss the individual notes they have written. Together, they try to begin to reconstruct the original text they heard.
4. Two pairs of students then join to make a group of four. They repeat the same process, again adding to and adapting their notes. By using these four sets of notes, the group will probably be able to produce a fairly accurate record of the original passage.
5. At this stage you can ask individual students to write out the passage based on their notes. Alternatively, the group can do it together. (Groups could use large sheets of paper and then put them on the wall for display.) Give them time to check their writing, such as grammar and spelling. Then put the original passage on an overhead and let the students compare what they have written with the original. The aim is not to produce an identical text to the original, but to produce a text that has the same information and is appropriately worded. Discuss with students the differences between the texts, pointing out (and praising) variations that make sense and that show how the students were using their language knowledge.

Note: At Steps 3, 4, and 5, encourage students to *reflect on* what they are writing (e.g., to use what they know about English grammar to check for grammatical errors; to ask the question "Does it make sense?"; and to use the context to guess words they were unable to hear). See Chapter 6.

* **During-Reading Activities**

These activities include the following: modeled reading; skimming and scanning activities; rereading for detail; shared book; word masking; pause and predict; shadow reading; summarizing the text; jigsaw reading; reading aloud. See Chapter 5.

✳ *Expert and Home Groups*

This is the organizational structure that underpins activities such as jigsaw listening or jigsaw reading. Divide students into groups of six. (Numbers can be varied depending on your class size.) Their task is to become "experts" in one aspect of a topic. Assign a letter or name to each group. Within each group, number the students from one through six. After they have become experts, through listening, viewing, reading, or other kinds of research, the groups reform in their "home" groups, this time with all the 1s together, all the 2s and so on. They share the information they have acquired, with each person contributing different information. In these kinds of activities, it's helpful to design information sheets for recording information. Students will fill in one part of the information in their expert group, and the remainder of the information on the basis of what they learn in their home group. See Chapters 2 and 4.

✳ *Find My Partner*

Students should each have five or six pictures; two are the same but the others differ in very small details. Mark one of the two identical pictures with a cross. Cards should be face down on the table. Each child in a group of five (or however many cards there are) takes one card. They must not show each other their pictures. The child who has the picture marked with a cross must ask questions of the others in the group to find out who has exactly the same picture. See Chapter 2.

✳ *Find the Difference*

This is a barrier game in which pairs of students have two similar but not identical pictures; they must find the differences by questioning each other and/or describing the picture. See Chapters 2 and 4.

✳ *Hands Up!*

Students have a set of questions based on a text. The text is read aloud, and as students hear the information that answers a question, they raise their hands. Make sure that the questions are in the order in which the information is given in the text. See Chapter 6.

✳ *Hot Seat*

This is a role-play activity that can involve the whole class. Children sit in a circle, with one student, who takes on a character role, sitting in the "hot seat." The remainder of the class ask the character in the hot seat questions about his or her life. The role can be based on a character in a book the class has read, or on a historical character. See Chapters 2 and 5.

✳ *If You Are . . .*

This is a listening activity that requires students to follow different instructions depending on other information that relates to them. See Chapter 6.

✳ *I'm Thinking of Something That . . .*

Each child in a small group must choose an object to describe from a set of pictures related to a topic being studied. Each student begins by saying "I'm thinking of something that . . ." and continues by describing the object. Other students must guess what is being described. See Chapter 2.

✳ *Information Extraction Tasks*

These are listening activities aimed at developing students' skills in listening for key information. See Chapter 6.

✳ *Information Grid*

This is an information transfer activity whereby information in a text is represented in another way. An information grid is illustrated in Figure G–2. The example is not yet completed—students will add information as they research further. Note that it encourages students to pick out main points from information, and it is very valuable as an information resource for writing. It also dissuades students from simply copying out large chunks from books when they do a project! See Chapter 4.

✳ *Inquiry and Elimination*

This activity helps develop reasoning skills and practices question forms. See Chapter 2.

✳ *Interviews*

This is a particularly valuable activity for ESL students, since it gives them an opportunity to interact formally with an adult other than their teacher, and with someone they don't know. For many students, this means learning a more formal register of English (see Chapter 1). Questions should be prepared beforehand, with discussion about what it is appropriate to ask, the most important questions to ask, and the way these questions should be asked. This is a good opportunity to discuss forms of address and other "politeness" issues. See Chapter 4.

✳ *Jigsaw Listening*

In this activity, groups of students each listen to an audiotape. There is different information on each tape, which all students will eventually need. For example, in the dinosaur topic described in Chapter 4, the students could answer the question, "Why

Dinosaur	When it lived	What it looked like	What it ate	Other features + interesting facts
ankylosaurus	70 mya	Big and heavy Bony plates on its head, neck, and a club at the end of the tail	only plants	As big and heavy as a tank
stegosaurus		Plates on its back— one or two rows but we're not sure Bony spikes on its tail		Plates were to control its temperature Called the stupidest dinosaur because its brain was only the size of a walnut!
tyrannosaurus	100 mya	Very short arms. They couldn't reach its mouth	meat	Very fierce
diplodocus		Very long. Long neck		The longest dinosaur, as long as 7 cars or 16 people. Lived in N. America

FIGURE G–2. *Information Grid*

did the dinosaurs disappear?" Four groups could each listen to one hypothesis: they grew too large to move or breed, new flowering plants poisoned them, their diet caused them to lay eggs that didn't hatch, a meteorite hit the earth. Each group takes notes about what they have learned. Then the groups regroup, with four students coming together who each have information about one of the hypotheses. They share this and now have a basis to answer the question. This is an example of the use of the expert/home grouping described earlier. See Chapter 6.

❊ *Jumbled Sentences*

Have the child dictate a sentence to you that relates to themselves or to a book that has been read. Write the sentence onto a strip of card and then cut it into words. The child must sort the words back into the correct order. As a simpler variant of this activity, the child could also have a copy of the complete sentence on a strip of card on which they match and place each of the individual words. See Chapter 5.

✳ **Map Games**

These are barrier games using incomplete maps that must be completed through questioning, or games involving the giving of directions using the maps. See Chapter 6.

✳ **Matching Game (Listening)**

This is a listening activity in which students must match a number of pictures to their descriptions, which are read aloud. See Chapter 6.

✳ **Minimal Pair Exercises**

These are designed to help children hear the difference between the phonemes of English. See Chapter 6.

✳ **Monster Cloze**

This is a variation of the traditional cloze and is a whole-class activity. Only the *title* of the passage is written on the board. The passage itself, however, consists of only the gaps. Students guess the missing words (in any order), and the teacher writes in any correct words in the appropriate gap. The task becomes progressively easier because once the sentences are partially completed, students should be able to predict the remaining words by using their knowledge of the topic and of English grammar. See Chapter 5.

✳ **Paired Problem Solving**

Two problems are involved, with pairs of students solving one of the problems. Pairs solving different problems come together and question each other about how each pair solved its problem, prior to attempting later to solve the same problem themselves. See Chapter 2.

✳ **Picture and Sentence Matching**

Jumble up a set of pictures and corresponding sentences. Children must match each picture to the appropriate sentence. This could be based on a book that is being read in class. See Chapter 5.

✳ **Picture Dictation**

This is a listening activity in which students have a number of individual pictures corresponding to a story. The story is read aloud, and as they listen, students must put the pictures into the right sequence. See Chapter 6.

✳ *Picture Sequencing*

Use a set of pictures that tell a simple story, or that illustrate a sequence, such as the life cycle of an insect. Individually, in pairs, or in groups, students put the pictures in an appropriate order and write the story or describe the sequence. A more challenging use of a picture sequence, and one that focuses more on spoken language, involves giving each student in a group one card (there should be the same number of students as there are picture cards). Tell the students not to show the others in their group their card. Each student describes his or her card (it doesn't matter who starts), and when they have all finished describing their cards, the group decides on the basis of the descriptions which card should come first, which second, and so on. On the basis of the order decided, each student puts his or her card down. For younger students and those very new to English, make sure that cards are placed from left to right. See Chapter 2.

✳ *Problem-Solving Activities*

Groups of children solve a problem through discussion, and then report back to the class about their solutions.

✳ *Questionnaires*

Questionnaires are a useful way to collect opinions on a topic, such as the "Local Issue" discussed in Chapter 7. Constructing the questions also involves a focus on both form and appropriate register. See Chapter 2.

✳ *Running Dictation*

This is a team game that can be a very noisy activity! Students should be in teams of about six. Before you begin, write a short text on a large sheet of paper, starting each sentence on a new line. Place the text on a wall somewhere outside the classroom (e.g., in a corridor outside the room). The first member of each team runs out of the class to the text and reads (and tries to remember) the first sentence. He or she runs back into the class and dictates it to his or her team, who write it down. When everyone in the team has finished writing, the second member of the team runs out, reads and memorizes the second sentence, returns, and dictates it. This continues until a team has completed the text. If a member forgets the sentence on the way back (this happens often!), he or she can go back and read it again, but of course time is lost if they do this. Point out to students that they should try to think about the meaning of their sentence—simply trying to memorize a sentence as a string of words is much harder than remembering something meaningful. However, make sure that you use a text that is within your students' capabilities to understand. See Chapter 4.

✳ **Say It Again**

This is a listening activity in which students "shadow" a character in a video. It provides practice in pronunciation, stress, and intonation. See Chapter 6.

✳ **Semantic Web**

A semantic web, sometimes called a Semantic Map, is a way of collecting and organizing information. Often this is carried out initially as a brainstorm, with students recalling what they already know about a subject and the words and concepts they associate with the key word (see Figure G–3). As the figure demonstrates, often these ideas will reflect very different categories and levels of generalization, so after the initial brainstorm, these random associations can be reorganized and classified by the teacher and students together. (For this reason, it helps to use small pieces of paper to write up the suggestions, fixed with reusable adhesive putty, which can be repositioned later.) The semantic map in Figure G–3 was later reorganized into four types of information: the names of some dinosaurs, some facts about them, why they became extinct, and how they have been used in fiction. As the topic progressed, new categories, subcategories, and information were added. See Chapter 4.

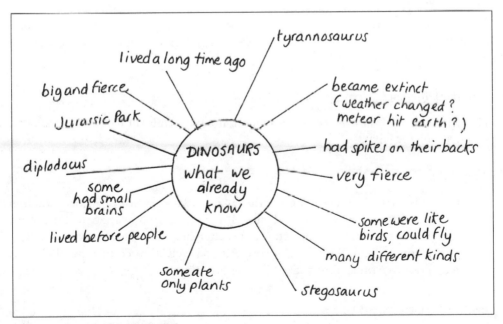

FIGURE G–3. *Initial Semantic Web*

❋ *Shadow Reading*

Children either follow or "read along" with an audiotaped excerpt from a book. The teacher can create this. If children read aloud, they should try to follow the pronunciation, stress patterns, and intonation patterns as closely as possible. This is a useful "rehearsal" if children are going to read aloud to the rest of the class (e.g., in Readers' Theatre). See Chapters 5 and 6.

❋ *Sound Bingo*

This is based on a traditional Bingo game. Children hear sounds rather than words. For example, they may hear a baby crying or a dog barking. As they hear the relevant word, they cover the appropriate word on the Bingo board, for example, *baby* or *dog*. See Chapter 6.

❋ *Sound Stories*

This is a listening activity in which children must find a connection between several sounds. See Chapter 6.

❋ *Split Dictation*

This is a listening activity in which pairs of students each have part of a text. By dictating the parts they have to their partner, each student must complete the text by filling in what is missing. See Chapter 6.

❋ *Spot the Difference*

This listening activity is aimed at developing students' skills in listening for general information. See Chapter 6.

❋ *Story Map*

A story map is a visual representation of the characters and events of a story. Children can construct this in groups or individually, either adding to it as they read the story, or developing it as an after-reading activity. It is often helpful to use a story map to help prompt students if they are retelling a story. Alternatively, they could draw their own story map prior to writing a story. See Chapter 5.

❋ *Teacher-Guided Reporting*

As a child retells about something he or she has learned or found out, the teacher provides scaffolding to support the child's retelling. To do so, the teacher uses prompting, asking for clarification, recasting, or questioning. See Chapters 2 and 3.

✳ **Text Reconstruction**

Students reconstruct a text that has been cut up into sentences or paragraphs. They should be able to explain the sequence they have chosen. This is a good activity for focusing on the cohesive links across sentences, such as pronoun reference and conjunctions. See Chapters 4 and 5.

✳ **Vanishing Cloze**

This is another cloze variation. Write up on the board a short passage (three or four sentences, or even shorter for beginners) based on something students are familiar with. Students read it aloud together. Erase one word from anywhere in the text. Students read it again, putting back the missing word. Erase another word and repeat the process. Continue until all the words are removed, so that students are now "reading" from memory. These repeated readings are especially helpful if the text contains a tricky grammatical structure or subject-specific vocabulary that the students are currently learning, since it provides a context for repetition that is both fun and challenging. See Chapter 5.

✳ **Wallpapering**

This is a brainstorm activity. Give groups of students small sheets of paper to write down one thing they know about a topic, or one idea they have about a controversial topic. Stick the pieces of paper on the walls of the classroom. Students walk round and read other students' ideas. Later they can comment on the ideas of others: *I agree with the one that said . . . I didn't know that . . . I don't think that's right.* See Chapter 4.

✳ **What Can You Hear?**

This is a listening activity designed to introduce students to focused listening. See Chapter 6.

✳ **What Did You See?**

This is a memory game that practices vocabulary. Learners must try to remember a selection of objects or pictures, which they look at for a short time, and which are then covered. See Chapter 2.

✳ **Word Linking**

This is an activity designed to improve pronunciation and listening skills. See Chapter 6.

✳ **Word Wall/Word Bank**

This is a display of words that are relevant to a particular topic or text type (see Figure G–4). See Chapter 4.

Connectives for discussion writing
First
Second
Also
In addition
On the other hand
However
Nevertheless
Therefore

Connectives for narratives	"Saying" verbs for narratives
One day	said
After	explained
Afterwards	shouted
Later on	growled
The following morning	cried
In the end	yelled
Finally	whispered
At last	replied

FIGURE G–4. *Word Wall/Word Bank*

For Further Practical Ideas

SCHINKE-LLANO, L., and R. RAUFF, eds. 1996. *New Ways in Teaching Young Children*. Alexandria, VA: Teachers of English to Speakers of Other Languages (TESOL).

SION, C., ed. 1991. *More Recipes for Tired Teachers: Well-Seasoned Activities for the ESOL Classroom*. New York: Addison-Wesley.

Bibliography

ADAMSON, H. 1993. *Academic Competence*. New York: Longman.

ALLEN, P., M. SWAIN, B. HARLEY, and J. CUMMINS. 1990. "Aspects of Classroom Treatment: Towards a More Comprehensive View of Second Language Education." In *The Development of Second Language Proficiency*, ed. B. Harley, P. Allen, J. Cummins, and M. Swain. Cambridge, UK: Cambridge University Press.

ANDERSON, R., and P. Pearson. 1984. "A Schema-Theoretic View of Basic Processes in Reading Comprehension." In *Handbook of Reading Research*, ed. P. Pearson. White Plains, NY: Longman.

BARNES, D. 1976. *From Communication to Curriculum*. Harmondsworth, UK: Penguin.

BAYNHAM, M. 1993. "Literacy in TESOL and ABE: Exploring Common Themes." *Open Letter* 2 (2): 4–16.

BOOMER, G. 1989. "Literacy: Beyond the Epic Challenge." Paper presented at the Joint Australian Reading Association and the Australian Association for the Teaching of English National Conference: *Across the Borders—Language at the Interface*, Darwin, AU.

BRANSFORD, J., and M. JOHNSON. 1972. "Contextual Prerequisites for Understanding: Some Investigations of Comprehension and Recall." *Journal of Verbal Learning and Verbal Behaviour* 11: 717–26.

BRICE-HEATH, S. 1983. *Ways with Words*. Cambridge, UK: Cambridge University Press.

BRUNER, J. 1978. "The Role of Dialogue in Language Acquisition." In *The Child's Conception of Language*, ed. A. Sinclair, R. Jarvella, and W. Levelt. New York: Springer-Verlag.

BRYANT, P., and L. BRADLEY. 1985. *Children's Reading Problems*. Oxford, UK: Blackwell.

CAMBOURNE, B. 1998. *The Whole Story: Natural Language and the Acquisition of Literacy in the Classroom*. Auckland, NZ: Ashton Scholastic.

CARRELL, P. 1988. "Interactive Text Processing: Implications for ESL/Second Language Reading Classrooms." In *Interactive Approaches to Second Language Reading*, ed. P. Carrell, J. Devine, and D. Eskey. Cambridge, UK: Cambridge University Press.

CHRISTIE, F. 1990. "The Changing Face of Literacy." In *Literacy for a Changing World*, ed. F. Christie. Hawthorn, Victoria, AU: ACER.

CLEGG, J., ed. 1996. *Mainstreaming ESL: Case Studies in Integrating ESL Students into the Mainstream Curriculum*. Clevedon, UK: Multilingual Matters.

COLLIER, V. 1989. "How Long? A Synthesis of Research in Academic Achievement in a Second Language." *TESOL Quarterly* 23: 509–31.

————. 1995. "Acquiring a Second Language for School." *Directions in Language and Education. National Clearing House of Bilingual Education* 1 (4): entire issue.

COOK, S. 1998. *Collaborative Learning Activities in the Classroom: Designing Inclusive Materials for Learning and Language Development*. Leicester, UK: Resource Centre for Multicultural Education.

CORSON, D. 1993. *Language, Minority Education and Gender*. Clevedon, UK: Multilingual Matters.

CREENAUNE, T., and L. ROWLES. 1996. *What's Your Purpose: Reading Strategies for Nonfiction Texts*. Sydney, AU: Primary English Teaching Association.

CUMMINS, J. 1996. *Negotiating Identities: Education for Empowerment in a Diverse Society*. Ontario, CA: California Association for Bilingual Education.

————. 2000. *Language, Power and Pedagogy: Bilingual Children in the Crossfire*. Clevedon, UK: Multilingual Matters.

CUMMINS, J., and D. SAYERS. 1995. *Brave New Schools: Challenging Cultural Illiteracy Through Global Learning Networks*. New York: St. Martin's Press.

DAVISON, C., and A. WILLIAMS. 2001. "Integrating Language and Content: Unresolved Issues." In *English as a Second Language in the Mainstream: Teaching, Learning and Identity*, ed. B. Mohan, C. Leung, and C. Davison. Harlow, UK: Longman.

DELPIT, L. 1988. "The Silenced Dialogue: Power and Pedagogy in Educating Other People's Children." *Harvard Educational Review* 58 (3): 280–98.

DEREWIANKA, B. 1990. *Exploring How Texts Work*. Portsmouth, NH: Heinemann.

DES-FOUNTAIN, J., and A. HOWE. 1992. "Pupils Working Together on Understanding." In *Thinking Voices: The Work of the National Literacy Project*, ed. K. Norman. London: Hodder and Stoughton.

DILLON, J. 1990. *The Practice of Questioning*. London: Routledge.

DRIVER, R. 1983. *The Pupil as Scientist?* Milton Keynes, UK: Open University Press.

EARNEST GARCIA, G. 1994. "Assessing the Literacy Development of Second-Language Students: A Focus on Authentic Assessment." In *Kids Come in All Languages: Reading Instruction for ESL Students*, ed. K. Spangenberg-Urbschat and R. Pritchard. Newark, DE: International Reading Association.

EDWARDS, D., and N. MERCER. 1987. *Common Knowledge: The Development of Understanding in the Classroom*. London: Methuen.

EHRI, L. 1990. "Development of the Ability to Read Words." In *Handbook for Reading Research* Vol. 12, ed. P. Pearson. New York: Longman.

ELLEY, W. 1984. "Exploring the Reading Difficulties of Second-Language Readers in Fiji." In *Reading in a Foreign Language*, ed. C. Alderson and A. Urquhart. London: Longman.

ELLIS, R. 1994. *The Study of Second Language Acquisition*. Oxford, UK: Oxford University Press.

FEEZ, S. 1995. "Systemic Functional Linguistics and Its Applications in Australian Language Education: A Short History." *Interchange* 27: 8–11.

FREIRE, P. 1983. "Banking Education." In *The Hidden Curriculum and Moral Education: Deception or Discovery?*, ed. H. Giroux and D. Purpel. Berkeley, CA: McCutcheon Publishing Corporation.

GARIBALDI ALLEN, V. 1994. "Selecting Materials for the Reading Instruction of ESL Children." In *Kids Come in All Languages: Reading Instruction for ESL Students*, ed. K. Spangenberg-Urbschat and R. Pritchard. Newark, DE: International Reading Association.

GIBBONS, P. 1992. "Identifying the Language Needs of Bilingual Learners." In *Language Assessment in Primary Classrooms*, ed. B. Derewianka. Sydney, AU: Harcourt Brace Jovanovich.

———. 1993. *Learning to Learn in a Second Language*. Portsmouth, NH: Heinemann.

———. 2001. "Learning a New Register in a Second Language." In *English Language Teaching in Its Social Context*, ed. C. Candlin and N. Mercer. New York: Routledge.

GOODMAN, K. 1967. "Reading: A Psycholinguistic Guessing Game." In *Language and Literacy: The Collected Writing of Kenneth S. Goodman. Vol 1: Process, Theory, Research*, ed. F. Gollasch. London: Routledge.

GOSWAMI, U., and P. BRYANT. 1990. *Phonological Skills and Learning to Read*. Hove, UK: Lawrence Erlbaum Associates.

GRAVES, D. 1983. *Writing: Teachers and Children at Work*. London: Heinemann.

HALLIDAY, M. 1975. *Learning How to Mean: Explorations in the Development of Language*. London: Arnold.

———. 1993. "Towards a Language-Based Theory of Learning." *Linguistics and Education* 5: 93–116.

———. "Three Aspects of Children's Language Development: Learning Language, Learning Through Language, Learning About Language." In *Oral and Written Language Development: Impact on Schools (Proceedings from the 1979 and 1980 IMPACT Conferences)*, ed. Y. Goodman, M. Hayssler, and D. Strickland. International Reading Association and National Council of Teachers. (No place or date) 7–19.

HALLIDAY, M., and R. HASAN. 1976. *Cohesion in English*. London: Longman.

KALANTZIS, M., B. COPE, G. NOBLE, and S. POYNTING. 1991. *Cultures of Schooling: Pedagogies for Cultural Difference and Social Access*. London: Falmer Press.

LUKE, A., and P. FREEBODY. 1990. "'Literacies' Programs: Debate and Demands in Cultural Context." *Prospect* 5 (3): 7–16.

MARTIN, J. 1984. "Language, Register and Genre." In *Children Writing: Study Guide*, ed. F. Christie. Geelong, Victoria, AU: Deakin University Press.

———. 1986. "Secret English: Discourse Technology in a Junior Secondary School." Paper presented at the *Language Socialisation Home and School Conference*. Proceedings from the *Working Conference on Language in Education*, Macquarie University, Sydney, AU.

———. 1989. "Technicality and Abstraction: Language for the Creation of Specialised Knowledge." In *Writing in Schools (B.Ed. Course Reader)*, ed. F. Christie. Geelong, Victoria, AU: Deakin University Press.

———. 1990. "Literacy in Science: Learning to Handle Literacy as Technology." In *Literacy for a Changing World*, ed. F. Christie. Hawthorn, Victoria, AU: ACER.

MARTIN, J., F. CHRISTIE, and J. ROTHERY. 1987. "Social Processes in Education: A Reply to Sawyer and Watson (and Others)." In *The Place of Genre in Learning: Current Debates*, ed. I. Reid. Geelong, Victoria, AU: Deakin University Press.

MARTIN, N., P. WILLIAMS, J. WILDING, S. HEMMINGS, and P. MEDWAY. 1976. *Understanding Children Talking*. London: Penguin.

MAYBIN, J., N. MERCER, and B. STIERER. 1992. "Scaffolding Learning in the Classroom." In *Thinking Voices, The Work of the National Oracy Project*, ed. K. Norman. London: Hodder and Stoughton.

McGROARTY, M. 1992. "Cooperative Learning: The Benefits for Content-Area Teaching." In *The Multicultural Classroom*, ed. P. Richard-Amato and M. Snow. New York: Longman.

———. 1993. "Cooperative Learning and Language Acquisition." In *Cooperative Learning: A Response to Linguistic and Cultural Diversity*, ed. D. Holt. Washington, DC: Center for Applied Linguistics.

McKAY, P., A. DAVIES, B. DEVLIN, J. CLAYTON, R. OLIVER, and S. ZAMMIT. 1997. *The Bilingual Interface Project Report*. Canberra, AU: Department of Employment, Education, Training and Youth Affairs.

MEHAN, B. 1979. *Learning Lessons*. Cambridge, MA: Harvard University Press.

MERCER, N. 1994. "Neo-Vygotskian Theory and Classroom Education." In *Language, Literacy and Learning in Educational Practice*, ed. B. Stierer and J. Maybin. Clevedon, UK: Multilingual Matters.

———. 1995. *The Guided Construction of Knowledge: Talk Amongst Teachers and Learners*. Clevedon, UK: Multilingual Matters.

———. 2000. *Words and Minds: How We Use Language to Think Together*. London: Routledge.

MOHAN, B. 1986. *Language and Content*. Reading, MA: Addison-Wesley.

———. 2001. "The Second Language as a Medium of Learning." In *English as a Second Language in the Mainstream: Teaching, Learning and Identity*, ed. B. Mohan, C. Leung, and C. Davison. London: Longman.

NUNAN, D. 1990. "Learning to Listen in a Second Language." *Prospect* 5 (2): 7–23.

NUNAN, D., and L. MILLER, eds. 1995. *New Ways in Teaching Listening*. Alexandria, VA: Teachers of English to Speakers of Other Languages (TESOL).

OAKES, J. 1985. *Keeping Track: How High Schools Structure Inequality*. New Haven, CT: Yale University Press.

PAINTER, C. 1984. *Into the Mother Tongue: A Case Study in Early Language Development*. London: Pinter.

———. 1985. *Learning the Mother Tongue*. Geelong, Victoria: Deakin University Press.

———. 1988. "The Concept of Genre." Paper commissioned by Queensland Department of Immigrant Education, Australia.

PICA, T. 1994. "Research on Negotiation: What Does It Reveal About Second Language Learning Conditions, Processes, and Outcomes?" *Language Learning* 44: 493–527.

PICA, T., R. YOUNG, and C. DOUGHTY. 1987. "The Impact of Interaction on Comprehension." *TESOL Quarterly* 21 (4): 737–58.

REYNOLDS, R., M. TAYLOR, M. STEFFENSEN, L. SHIREY, and R. ANDERSON. 1981. "Cultural Schemata and Reading Comprehension." In *Center for the Study of Reading Technical Report No. 201*: Urbana-Champaign, IL.

RICHARDS, J., and R. HURLEY. 1990. "Language and Content: Approaches to Curriculum Alignment." In *The Language Teaching Matrix*, ed. J. Richards. Cambridge, UK: Cambridge University Press.

RIGG, P., and V. ALLEN, eds. 1989. *When They Don't All Speak English: Integrating the ESL Student in the Regular Classroom*. Urbana, IL: National Council of Teachers of English.

ROST, M. 1991. *Listening in Action*. New York: Prentice Hall.

ROTHERY, J. 1992. "Assessing Children's Writing." In *Language Assessment in Primary Classrooms*, ed. B. Derewianka. London: Harcourt Brace Jovanovich.

ROWE, M. 1986. "Wait Time: Slowing Down May Be a Way of Speeding Up." *Journal of Teacher Education* 37: 43–50.

SCHINKE-LLANO, L., and R. RAUFF, eds. 1996. *New Ways in Teaching Young Children*. Alexandria, VA: Teachers of English to Speakers of Other Languages (TESOL).

SHORT, D. 1993. "Assessing Integrating Language and Content." *TESOL Quarterly* 27 (4): 627–56.

SINCLAIR, J., and R. COULTHARD. 1975. *Towards an Analysis of Discourse: The English Used by Teachers and Pupils*. London: Oxford University Press.

SION, C., ed. 1991. *More Recipes for Tired Teachers: Well-Seasoned Activities for the ESOL Classroom*. New York: Addison-Wesley.

STEFFENSON, M., C. JOAG-DEV, and R. ANDERSON. 1979. "A Cross-Cultural Perspective on Reading Comprehension." *Reading Research Quarterly* 15 (1): 10–29.

SWAIN, M. 1995. "Three Functions of Output in Second Language Learning." In *Principle and Practice in Applied Linguistics: Studies in Honour of H. G. Widdowson*, ed. G. Cook and B. Seidlehofer. Oxford, UK: Oxford University Press.

THOMAS, W., and V. COLLIER. 1999. *School Effectiveness for Language Minority Students*. George Washington University, Washington, DC: National Clearinghouse for Bilingual Education.

VAN LIER, L. 1996. *Interaction in the Language Curriculum: Awareness, Autonomy and Authenticity*. London: Longman.

VYGOTSKY, L. 1978. *Mind in Society: The Development of Higher Psychological Processes*. London: Harvard University Press.

———. 1986. *Thought and Language*. Ed. and trans. A Kozulin. Cambridge, MA: Harvard University Press.

WAJNRYB, R. 1990. *Grammar Dictation*. Oxford, UK: Oxford University Press.

WALLACE, C. 1988. *Learning to Read in a Multicultural Society: The Social Context of Second Language Literacy*. New York: Prentice Hall.

————. 1992. *Reading*. Oxford, UK: Oxford University Press.

WEGERIF, R., and N. MERCER. 1996. "Computers and Reasoning Through Talk in the Classroom." *Language and Education* 10 (1): 47–64.

WELLS, G. 1999. "Language and Education: Reconceptualising Education as Dialogue." *Annual Review of Applied Linguistics* (19): 135–55.

————. 2000. "Dialogic Inquiry in Education: Building on the Legacy of Vygotsky." In *Vygotskian Perspectives on Literacy Research: Constructing Meaning Through Collaborative Inquiry*, ed. C. Lee and P. Smagorinsky. Cambridge, UK: Cambridge University Press.

WILLIAMS, G. 1999. "Grammar as a Semiotic Tool in Child Literacy Development." In *Language Teaching: New Insights for the Language Teacher Series 40*, ed. C. Ward and W. Renandya. Singapore: Regional Language Centre: SEAMO.

WONG-FILLMORE, L. 1985. "When Does Teacher Talk Work as Input?" In *Input in Second Language Acquisition*, ed. S. Gass and C. Madden. Rowley, MA: Newbury House.

WOOD, D., J. BRUNER, and G. ROSS. 1976. "The Role of Tutoring in Problem Solving." *Journal of Child Psychology and Psychiatry* 17 (2): 89–100.

Index